# 3-MINUTE DEVOTIONS

## from the Proverbs

## Wisdom for Women

© 2018 by Barbour Publishing, Inc.

Devotional writing by Joan C. Webb in association with Snapdragon Groups, Tulsa, Oklahoma, USA.

Prayers by MariLee Parrish.

ISBN 978-1-68322-711-3

Published by Barbour Books, an imprint of Barbour Publishing, Inc., 1810 Barbour Drive, Uhrichsville, Ohio 44683, www.barbourbooks.com

*Our mission is to inspire the world with the life-changing message of the Bible.*

Member of the
Evangelical Christian
Publishers Association

Printed in the United States of America.

# 3-MINUTE
# DEVOTIONS
from the *Proverbs*

## *Wisdom for Women*

BARBOUR BOOKS
An Imprint of Barbour Publishing, Inc.

# Introduction

*My [daughter], if you accept my words and store
up my commands within you, turning your ear to wisdom
and applying your heart to understanding, indeed, if you
call out for insight and cry aloud for understanding, and
if you look for it as for silver and search for it as for hidden
treasure, then you will understand the fear of the L*ORD
*and find the knowledge of God. For the L*ORD *gives wisdom;
from his mouth come knowledge and understanding.*

PROVERBS 2:1-6 NIV

What a remarkable opportunity you have! Imagine becoming a wise, knowledgeable, and discerning woman—whether you have one, two, or zero degrees. Regardless of your age, position, or season, you're invited to walk with and learn from the source of all wisdom, God Himself. He knows you better than you know yourself, and He cares—about your secret dreams, financial struggles, career woes, and family dynamics.

*3-Minute Devotions from the Proverbs* was created to help you develop a richer relationship with our awesome God and give you a glimpse of His knowledge on the life topics that concern you. Our prayer is that while reading these words, you'll grow to recognize your options, make wise daily choices, and take intentional action. That's what God wants for you. Now isn't that amazing?

# A Wise Woman

*Don't jump to conclusions—there may be a perfectly*
*good explanation for what you just saw.*
PROVERBS 25:8 MSG

You cry at movies; your sister doesn't. Your husband shares openly with anyone he meets; you prefer to take time getting to know someone first. You enjoy working alone; your boss works best on a team. Your mother gives instant solutions; you like mulling over the options. It's easy to jump to conclusions when another person doesn't think or act as you do. But when you suspend judgment of the differing ideas and opinions of others, you're a wise—and gracious—woman.

*Heavenly Father, help me to stop my constant judging.*
*You've created all of us different for Your purposes.*
*Fill me with Your love and graciousness toward others.*

# *Splashes*

*To get wisdom is to love oneself;*
*to keep understanding is to prosper.*

PROVERBS 19:8 NRSV

If you can accept yourself, you will probably be able to more readily accept the idiosyncrasies of others. If you are patient with yourself, you will almost certainly be more tolerant toward your loved ones. If you have learned to forgive yourself, you're likely to find you can more easily forgive someone else. Self-respect increases as you stay committed to gaining a heart of wisdom. This attitude splashes onto your other relationships, and acceptance gradually becomes a way of life.

*Father, let me see myself as You see me. I'm covered with the righteousness of Christ. I'm forgiven, free, and dearly loved. Help me to extend this mind-set to those around me.*

# *You're a Star!*

*The ways of right-living people glow with light;
the longer they live, the brighter they shine.*

PROVERBS 4:18 MSG

A ging isn't for wimps! It's true. Whether you're twenty-five or seventy-five, there are probably things about getting older that you don't appreciate. Extra pounds. Hormone imbalances. Another gray hair. Yet, as a God-honoring woman, you probably have one thing that only grows more beautiful and amazing with age—a heart of wisdom. The longer you live and the more wisdom you accumulate, the brighter your influence. So congratulate yourself. You're not a wimp, you're a star.

*Father, thank You for choosing me to be Your light
while I walk this earth. Let me radiate Your love
and goodness to others all the days of my life.*

## *Glorious*

---

*The glory of the young is their strength; the gray
hair of experience is the splendor of the old.*

PROVERBS 20:29 NLT

The expression "Generation Gap" became popular in the
1960s, although it probably existed in some uncoined
sense throughout history. Young people don't get their
grandparents, and the over-fifty crowd can't figure out
their juniors. Some sense a standoff. But the truth is, there
is beauty on both sides of the gap. Young people possess
stamina and a lust for life, while those who've been around
awhile are reservoirs of experience and wisdom. In God,
we are glorious at any age.

---

*Lord God, allow me to see the hearts of all people instead
of our differences. Help me to move boldly toward everyone
You put on my path no matter their age or stage in life.*

## Cultivating Beauty

*Humans are satisfied with whatever looks good;*
*God probes for what is good.*
PROVERBS 16:2 MSG

Like many women, you probably enjoy looking nice when you go out for a special occasion. You want a hairstyle that flatters your face, clothes that fit well, and a little makeup to enhance your eyes and cheeks. God likes it when you feel good about your appearance. Still though, He cares more about the inner you. He wants to cultivate what's good about you socially, emotionally, mentally, and spiritually. Join with Him in cultivating the beauty that's inside you.

*You created me in Your image, God, and I'm so thankful!*
*Let the glow on my face and the twinkle in my eyes come*
*from a heart that knows Your love and faithfulness.*

## Pure Motives

*We justify our actions by appearances;*
*GOD examines our motives.*
PROVERBS 21:2 MSG

People—women and men—want to look good to others. Sometimes we do this by name-dropping, pretending we don't need help, or reciting our credentials and achievements. At other times we do it by being overly nice, overworking, and rarely saying no. Both approaches to trying to keep our appearances up can wear us out. Relief comes when you admit your need, allow God to purify your motives, and then just enjoy honoring Him as the person He created you to be.

*God, I ask You to examine my heart. Show me anything*
*that is hindering me from a more authentic relationship*
*with You and those around me. I want to honor You!*

## More Than You Know

*The LORD directs our steps, so why try to*
*understand everything along the way?*
PROVERBS 20:24 NLT

Are you tired of trying so hard to make sure you do everything just right? Do you long to hear God whispering that He's with you and in control? Then you're like many other busy and overworked women. God knows your desire to love others, serve, and make wise choices. He hears your genuine prayer for help and strength. And He's answering. So lean back and take a deep breath. You are loved more than you'll ever know.

*Please increase my faith, Lord. I want to believe*
*that You are who You say You are! You are with me and*
*guiding me with each step. Help me to trust You more.*

# Give Your Doubt Away

*The LORD will be your confidence and will
keep your foot from being caught.*
PROVERBS 3:26 NRSV

Life is risky. With these risks come adventure, fulfillment—and uncertainty. Are you starting a career and overwhelmed with all you must learn? Are you a new mother, wondering how you'll raise this tiny person who awakens you in the night? Although you enjoy your independence, do you wonder whether you'll ever find a mate? Are you facing big decisions now that your husband is gone? Whatever your challenge, give your doubt to God. He'll never leave you. Never.

*I lay my doubts at Your feet today, Lord. I want You
to be the Lord of my life. Not just my Savior but my
Counselor, my ever-present friend, and my safe haven.*

# Be Authentic

*The LORD looks deep inside people and
searches through their thoughts.*

PROVERBS 20:27 NCV

If you're like most women who've participated in relationship surveys, you want someone to hear your heart and not be frightened off. Although you've been disappointed in relationships before, you still desire to be loved for who you really are. Good news! God is not surprised by what you feel, say, or think. He knows you inside and out and loves you just the way you are. So drop your guard and be authentic with Him. He isn't going anywhere.

*I'm amazed that You see me, God! You are at work in
my heart and know me better than I know myself.
Continue to show me who You are as I open my heart to You.*

## Ask Him

---

*People's thoughts can be like a deep well, but someone*
*with understanding can find the wisdom there.*

PROVERBS 20:5 NCV

People have their own answers—or can at least find them.
This is a basic tenet of the highly successful industry
of life coaching. Life coaches ask powerful questions that
help their clients discover those hidden answers, move
past their status quo, and grow. You have your own answers
too. They may be lodged deep within you, but with some
authentic sharing and a wise companion's thoughtful
probing, you can find the wisdom. Ask God to direct you
to this kind of authenticity.

---

*You are my Counselor and my source of wisdom, Lord.*
*Reveal the thoughts and attitudes of my heart*
*so that I can grow in truth and freedom.*

# Discover Balance

*Do you like honey? Don't eat too much,*
*or it will make you sick!*

PROVERBS 25:16 NLT

"All work and no play makes Jack a dull boy." (By the way, all work and no play can make Jill a dull girl as well!) You've probably heard this age-old axiom countless times. Yet the opposite is also true. All play and no work makes Jack and Jill uninteresting, not to mention unproductive. Focusing on one area of life to the detriment of its counterpoint is not wise. You can discover balance and thrive.

*Lord, align my heart with Your will for my life.*
*Help me to find the balance I need to live a*
*meaningful and productive life as I follow You.*

# Capable Woman

*She gets up before dawn to prepare breakfast for her household and plan the day's work for her servant girls.*

<small>PROVERBS 31:15 NLT</small>

You've got a lot to do. Each of your roles shouts for attention. How can you do it all? You can't. You're only one woman, although a caring, capable one. As a new employee, first-time mother, or start-up business owner, you encounter huge learning curves. You'll need to make adjustments. You may need to wake up early or ask for specialized help. This phase won't last forever. Give yourself a break. Do what you need to do to maintain balance.

*Your Word tells me that You've given me everything I need for life and godliness. It's through Your power alone that I can accomplish what You've set before me.*

# Lovely Wisdom

*"She'll garland your life with grace,
she'll festoon your days with beauty."*

PROVERBS 4:9 MSG

Y_ou are a beautiful creation of God. As a woman with a heart for God, you seek wisdom and understanding, and it shows. Grace reflects in your eyes as you speak with kindness and encouragement. Magazine advertisements and Hollywood may tell you that to be one of the "beautiful people" you must maintain an ideal weight, banish wrinkles, schedule regular pedicures, highlight your hair—and more. While all these regimens are fine, wisdom's loveliness in you far exceeds them all.

*Fill my heart with radiance that comes from
Your love, Lord God. I ask for wisdom and
grace to be the beauty that others see in me.*

# Praiseworthy Woman

*Charm is deceitful and beauty is passing,*
*but a woman who fears the LORD, she shall be praised.*
PROVERBS 31:30 NKJV

Do you ever feel society's pressure to look younger than your years? Dress in the season's latest fashions? Be your neighborhood's most charming hostess? Perhaps you sense this pressure and so you keep trying. Or maybe you've given up. Surely you've noticed that birthdays are inevitable, outer beauty can fade, and charm can fool. But be encouraged today. As you continue to honor, respect, and love God, you become a praiseworthy woman. Are you smiling yet?

*Lord, make me truly thankful for the woman that*
*You created me to be. Let me live to praise You,*
*heavenly Father. I delight myself in You.*

# Perfect Blessing

*The blessing of the LORD makes one rich.*
PROVERBS 10:22 NKJV

God blesses His children. No doubt about it. Just look around you. Your life is richer because of His protection, provision, presence, grace, and love. How can you respond to God's blessing? Gratefully accept Him and all that He gives you. And then bless Him back. Perhaps that seems like the ultimate audacity. The perfect Blesser receiving blessings from His own creation? Yet out of your rich inner resources of blessing, you can honor, revere, and bless the Giver.

*I bless Your name, heavenly Father! I praise and honor You for who You are and what You've done. I praise You for all the ways You've protected and led me. Thank You!*

## Build Up

---

*By the blessing of the upright a city is exalted.*
PROVERBS 11:11 NRSV

You may not know it, but you have the power to make a significant difference in your neighborhood, city, state, and—consequently—the world. What you believe about life, how you express those beliefs, how you treat your neighbors, acquaintances, governmental leaders, and coworkers reaches further than you may realize. When you bless those around you with your God-given wisdom, you are building up yourself, those around you, and gradually the world you live in.

---

*Father, show me what it means to bring Your kingdom to others—right here and now on this earth. You've given me much to do. Shine Your life and love through me.*

## Boundaries

*"I, Wisdom, live together with good judgment. . . .*
*I was there when he set the limits of the seas,*
*so they would not spread beyond their boundaries."*
PROVERBS 8:12, 29 NLT

Wisdom originates with God. When God designed the world, wisdom watched with joy as He drew distinct boundaries around the oceans and seas to protect His other creation from drowning. It's a picture of the boundaries He designed for you. You are not your mother. You are not your friend. You are not your spouse. No one has a right to step over your boundary line and take advantage of you. You are distinct. God made you that way.

*Thank You for creating me so wonderfully with distinct*
*boundaries and purpose. My life is Yours, Lord. Give me*
*wisdom to interact with others the way You designed me to.*

# Respond Wisely

*When you find a friend, don't outwear your welcome;*
*show up at all hours and he'll soon get fed up.*
PROVERBS 25:17 MSG

We all want to be loved and accepted. Yet some of us try too hard to make and keep friends. We may work harder than necessary to hold on to a boyfriend. We disregard boundaries, becoming overly enmeshed in another's life to the detriment of our own development. But there's good news. By placing your dependence on God first, you can change. Although transformation won't happen overnight, God will help you to respond wisely to the people in your life. Just ask Him.

*Jesus, help me to take my cues from You in relationships.*
*Please help me to be wise as I make and keep friendships.*
*Infuse my relationships with freedom, grace, and truth.*

# *Honorable*

---

*[God] loves it when business is aboveboard.*
PROVERBS 11:1 MSG

Whether you're a stay-at-home mother, empty nester, CEO, student, teacher, or attorney, God expects you to be honest in all your transactions—at the grocery store, the local bank, with your children and husband, in the boardroom, in court, on your tax forms, and when interacting with your repairman. Maybe you had trustworthy role models when you were growing up; perhaps you didn't. But as an aspiring wise woman, you can keep your everyday business dealings honorable. God will help.

---

*Lord, please cultivate my heart to become a woman of integrity. Teach me to see that all my actions and transactions can be good, honest work—work that honors You.*

## Trusting

*A prudent person foresees danger
and takes precautions.*

PROVERBS 22:3 NLT

Wisdom means planning for the worst, anticipating the best, and trusting God with every outcome. Whether you're researching colleges to attend, purchasing a home, getting married, starting a new company, taking care of your aging parents, or have just learned you're pregnant, you'll want to ask intelligent questions and plan for your next steps. God encourages you to think ahead. Seek the advice of trusted friends and associates, take necessary precautions, and then turn the results over to Him.

*Heavenly Father, I need Your wisdom as I plan
for the future. Help me to see my life as Yours.
I trust You to help me make the next wise choice.*

# Be Encouraged

*The diligent find freedom in their work.*
PROVERBS 12:24 MSG

It's fun watching a juggler. He tosses and balances balls, knives, hats, and sometimes flaming torches. It appears easy. Yet if you asked, you'd probably discover how many focused and diligent hours he practices. Learning to work without the constant buzz of busyness is like learning a juggling act. Although you want to stop rushing, it feels so impossible that you're tempted to cease trying. But be encouraged. You'll find success if you stay committed to practicing a balanced schedule.

*Father, teach me to be diligent as I seek Your will for my life. Show me what's important and where I need to persevere. Help me to find balance as I live out Your purposes.*

# Enjoy Every Minute

*One who moves too hurriedly misses the way.*
PROVERBS 19:2 NRSV

Hurry. Faster. Accomplish more. Learn this. Study that. Time's wasting. Do more for God. Messages like these fly around us daily—whether they're blatant or inferred. Perhaps you've sensed the rush and have become too busy, trying to do it all. Now you're tired. How can you change? First, know that God isn't the one pressing the HURRY button. He doesn't want you to dash through life and lose your way. He wants you to slow down and enjoy every minute.

*Father, please change my heart and actions*
*from striving to do everything that seems good,*
*to seeking Your presence in every moment.*

## Partner with God

*Foolish people lose their tempers,*
*but wise people control theirs.*

PROVERBS 29:11 NCV

Feeling angry doesn't automatically mean you've sinned. Anger is a normal response to injustice and wrong. God becomes angry over the disobedience of the people He loves. Jesus responded angrily to the corrupt money changers in the temple, but He didn't sin. It's when anger is allowed to rage or fester as resentment that it wreaks havoc with your soul and relationships. You're wise when you face your anger responsibly, discover its roots, and partner with God to control it.

*Lord, I bring all of my angry feelings to You.*
*Help me to sort them out. Show me the next*
*steps to take so that I honor You with my actions.*

# Walk Away

*A wise person stays calm when insulted.*

PROVERBS 12:16 NLT

It's difficult to remain calm when criticized, whether the criticism is legitimate or not. On occasion someone may unjustly criticize you merely for the thrill of creating chaos or starting a quarrel. It's not a wise way for them to interact, but it's not your problem. It's theirs. You don't have to fix them or engage in an argument. You can tell them calmly and firmly that you won't tolerate their disrespect. Then walk away with your head held high.

*Jesus, please help me to see others as You see them, even in the midst of confrontation. Give me wisdom to remember who I am in You when I'm faced with relational difficulties.*

# Growing Character

*Good character is the best insurance.*
PROVERBS 11:6 MSG

You can't know the future—even what will happen an hour from now. So you do what you can to protect yourself and your family and then give your tomorrows to God. Some things are not within your control. Yet it is always within your power to grow spiritually. You can choose to pray, read God's Word, and listen to His Spirit's gentle direction. As you do, you'll learn who He is, and He'll graciously develop love, patience, gentleness, and wisdom in you.

*Fill me with the fruits of Your Spirit, Lord. I give You full access to my heart. Plant and grow good fruit in me so that I faithfully trust You with all of life's questions.*

# Godly Attributes

*Moral character makes for smooth traveling.*
PROVERBS 11:5 MSG

You may have heard this expression before: "Character counts!" Choosing to invest your time and energy in cultivating a sense of fairness, compassion, wisdom, and respect for life and God enhances your chances for contentment. How you live affects not only you but also those you love. Perhaps you lacked good role models as a child. This is your opportunity to start a new trend. What godly attribute would you like to develop this year? No doubt about it, you'll enjoy the benefits.

*Lord Jesus, I invite You to look into my heart
and show me anything that needs changing.
Cultivate Your character inside of me.*

# Reach Out

*She opens her arms to the poor
and extends her hands to the needy.*

PROVERBS 31:20 NIV

Family, home, job, church, friends, school, personal and spiritual development—these fill your days. No doubt, like many other women, you find it difficult to become involved in long-term charity projects. Although you long to help, you only have so much time, energy, and money to go around. You can't do everything, but you can do something. Ask God to help you establish how, where, and when you can reach out to the hurting people in your world.

*Father, I ask You to show me the specific projects
You want me to get involved in. I know You will
provide every resource when I step out in faith.*

## A Richer Life

*Happy are those who are kind to the poor.*

PROVERBS 14:21 NRSV

A wise leader once said that you make a living by what you get—and you make a life by what you give. You receive a blessing when you give a blessing. As you develop wisdom, God expands your compassion for the poor. He smiles when you lovingly share with those who can't help themselves. And out of your gracious generosity springs joy. Your own life grows richer when you reach out in kindness to the disadvantaged.

*Open my eyes to see those in need around me, Father. Give me a nudge to help others when and where You want me to.*

## *God-Honoring Life*

*A refusal to correct is a refusal to love;*
*love your children by disciplining them.*
PROVERBS 13:24 MSG

You want your children to make wise choices. You send them to the best school you can afford. You take them to church. You expect their teachers to instruct them well. And as their mother, you have the personal privilege of sharing what you've learned about living a God-honoring life. You show how much you love your children when you graciously tell and show them what is right and wrong in God's sight.

*Heavenly Father, please give me Your*
*heart for my children. Give them a simple*
*understanding that they receive God-honoring*
*discipline because they are well-loved.*

# Choices

*Train up a child in the way he should go,*
*and when he is old he will not depart from it.*

PROVERBS 22:6 NKJV

Jesus promised that anyone who believes in Him will live forever. Paul wrote that we'll experience peace when we give our worries to God. Yet the pithy sayings in Proverbs aren't really promises. They're principles for wise living. One principle indicates that when your children are instructed and have seen that instruction modeled in your life, it becomes second nature to them. And when your children grow older, they will continue to make God-honoring choices.

*You've given me wise principles to live by, Lord. I know*
*You care about the choices I make. Allow my children*
*to see and know how close You are to each of us.*

## Doors of Opportunity

*Commit your works to the LORD,*
*and your thoughts will be established.*
PROVERBS 16:3 NKJV

When you don't understand all that's happening and aren't certain what to do next, honor your initial commitment to God. Continue with what God has shown you in the light or in less-confusing times. Do what is in front of you to do—without retreating into an isolating fear-maze. Although you may not know what your long-term future holds, walk through the doors of opportunity that open each day. In time God will establish your thoughts and clarify your path.

*Lord, I ask that You create in me a deep and abiding faith.*
*I want to trust You with every question and situation*
*that comes my way. Show me the next step to take.*

## Committed

*Commit yourself to instruction;*
*listen carefully to words of knowledge.*
PROVERBS 23:12 NLT

As a wise woman, you avoid succumbing to victim mentality. You no longer believe that you have little or zero choice in life. You stop saying yes when you really mean no. You cease doing for others what they can do for themselves. Realizing that the other person has the right to say no, you feel comfortable asking for what you need anyway. You seek advice, gain knowledge, and remain committed to personal and spiritual growth. Congratulations, wise woman!

*Father, mold me into a wise woman whose heart is*
*set on You. Give me the healthy boundaries I need*
*to live life in freedom as I commit my life to You.*

# Direct and Honest

*An open, face-to-face meeting results in peace.*
PROVERBS 10:10 MSG

Perhaps growing up you learned that it's more loving to avoid honest communication than to share what you really feel, think, or need. Maybe it was easier to blame—or to relay messages through someone else rather than deliver them yourself. Now you notice this approach fails to bring the results you desire. Sharing directly and honestly while encouraging others to do the same allows peace to flow into your relationships. Ask God for help in developing this wise communication skill.

*Confrontation is so hard for me, Lord. Would You change my attitude to view face-to-face meetings as divine appointments used to encourage one another?*

## Empowered

*As a tree gives fruit, healing words give life.*
PROVERBS 15:4 NCV

"Sticks and stones may break my bones, but words will never hurt me." Perhaps you're familiar with this often-repeated phrase. But is it true? Research shows that vicious teasing or persistent shaming and bullying can cause low self-esteem and even depression. On the flip side, encouraging, kind words heal and uplift. Just as a well-watered tree produces nourishing fruit, you nurture others when you listen, reflect, and empower them with your words.

*Heavenly Father, I know how important words are to You. Please give me wisdom as I bring life—not death or discouragement—to others with my words.*

# Words of Grace

*Watch your words and hold your tongue;*
*you'll save yourself a lot of grief.*
PROVERBS 21:23 MSG

Some of you tend to say almost anything that pops into your mind. This leads to laughter and rollicking conversation. You're the life of the party. Your quieter friends may envy your boldness. Yet sometimes you utter an excited comment and inadvertently hurt someone and cause yourself grief. God doesn't want to change your effervescent personality. He's the One who made you—and your more reserved friend. He only wants to temper your thoughts and words to grace others.

*Lord, please set a guard over my mouth and help*
*me to speak wisely, even when I'm joking with*
*friends. Show me how to speak with love and joy.*

# Think First

*The wise measure their words.*
PROVERBS 10:19 MSG

You measure the amount of sugar you add when making a cake. You measure the window frame when sewing a curtain. But have you measured your words lately? Too many sugary words may seem like flattery instead of genuine praise. Neglect to plan your comments before introducing a new concept at work and what you say may not fit. You don't have to be hypervigilant about your conversations, but it's wise to think before you speak. Ask God for direction.

*Lead me when I'm speaking, Lord. Help me to be sensitive to Your Spirit and the needs of others when it's my turn to share my thoughts and ideas.*

# Wise Counsel

*Without good direction, people lose their way; the more*
*wise counsel you follow, the better your chances.*

PROVERBS 11:14 MSG

Have you ever thought you knew the way to an appointment destination only to discover you were driving in the opposite direction? Frustrating, isn't it? Asking a reliable source for directions to follow greatly reduces your chances of ending up at an unwanted destination. Likewise, it's a sensible idea to pause and seek help when you feel lost in a relationship, with your job, or in your spiritual life. Following wise counsel enhances your chances for fulfillment, success, and growth.

*Heavenly Father, would You bring life-giving and*
*wise older friends into my life whom I can trust?*
*I need wise counsel from women who love You.*

## Give and Receive

*The heartfelt counsel of a friend is
as sweet as perfume and incense.*
PROVERBS 27:9 NLT

Picture yourself walking through a forest filled with fresh-smelling pine trees, tending the fragrant rose bushes in your front yard, or strolling down the aisles of your favorite bath and body lotions store. Sweet aromas; pleasant thoughts. Just as sweet is the loving counsel of a trusted friend. You don't have to be the one always advising. You don't have to be the one continually on the receiving end either. Good friends give and receive advice from one another.

*Lord, help me to listen when it's time to listen
and speak up when a friend needs good advice.
Plant Your wisdom in my heart as I give and receive.*

## *Closer*

---

*Who but God goes up to heaven and comes back down?*
*Who holds the wind. . . ? Who wraps up the oceans in his*
*cloak? Who has created the whole wide world?*

PROVERBS 30:4 NLT

Every thinking woman is responsible for her conclusions concerning the origin of our vast universe. Whether she insists God does or does not exist, she develops a belief system. Science invites you to view and study life's extraordinary complexities, the structural design inherent in each cell and how it all works together so intentionally. A wise woman like you will conclude that instead of pushing God out of the picture, this investigation pulls Him closer.

---

*God, help me to press in and search out the questions*
*I have about life and creation and science. I invite*
*Your Spirit to teach me Your truths without fear.*

## Behind It All

*By wisdom the LORD laid the earth's foundations,
by understanding he set the heavens in place;
by his knowledge the watery depths were divided,
and the clouds let drop the dew.*

PROVERBS 3:19-20 NIV

You may sometimes encounter people who don't know God as the all-powerful Creator. Perhaps you've been told by these people that evolution is the only intelligent explanation to believe and that religion should have no place in our educational system or in the study of science. Be kind, but refuse to be intimidated. You possess a deeper, more inspired wisdom that allows you to look beyond the smallness of the human mind and see the God behind it all.

*I ask that You protect my thought life when others challenge my beliefs, Lord. Allow me to show the truth of who You are by my life instead of angry, defensive words.*

## His Delight

*A good person basks in the delight of GOD.*
PROVERBS 12:2 MSG

Don't you love it when a friend says, "It was a delight to be with you"? You feel warm inside just knowing that someone you like likes you back. God likes you too. Really. In fact, He delights in you. You've been made delightful in His sight through Jesus' death and resurrection. You may already know that God loves you. After all, that's His nature. But also remember that He likes you—you are His delight.

*I delight myself in You, Lord, and You take delight in me. Thanks for filling me with Your love and liking who You made me to be!*

## *Consistently*

*Those who act faithfully are his delight.*

PROVERBS 12:22 NRSV

God can be trusted to follow through on His word. He consistently loves you, your family, and all His creation. Each day He rolls out the sun, gives the birds their song, waters the grass with dew, and encourages gravity to keep you grounded. Every gift God gives is wrapped in truth, grace, and honor. That's who He is. And He loves it when you faithfully reflect His character in everyday life. No doubt about it, He delights in you.

*Father, I'm so thankful for the gifts You have given
me and continue to bless me with each day.
You bring me great joy in Your presence.*

# Ant's Lesson

*Look at an ant. Watch it closely; let it teach you....*
*Nobody has to tell it what to do. All summer it stores up*
*food; at harvest it stockpiles provisions.*
PROVERBS 6:6–8 MSG

When you see a line of ants traveling across your kitchen counter, it's not really a welcome sight. Yet ants model a few worthwhile lessons about how to accomplish everyday tasks. First, ants self-motivate. They don't need someone to push them or direct their every step. Also, ants do the task at hand without procrastination. They diligently work until they've completed each job. What wise lesson will you take from the ant today?

*Father, thanks for giving me life lessons in the world*
*You created. You never stop teaching and leading*
*me...I just need to look around and listen!*

## Never Out of Style

*Diligent work gets a warm commendation.*
PROVERBS 14:35 MSG

Perhaps when you've been job hunting, you've voiced this question: "What do employers really want?" If so, you've probably heard something like this: "Companies hire people who are dependable, positive, flexible, honest, self-motivated, loyal, teachable, and willing to work hard and smart." Sounds like what wise King Solomon wrote about so long ago. Wisdom starts with God and produces credibility whether in the kitchen, office, or serving at church. Remember, your diligence never goes out of style.

*Remind me that when I do my job, Lord, I'm working
first and foremost to honor You and not man.
Every task I complete can be an act of worship.*

## Trail Guide

*The human mind plans the way,*
*but the LORD directs the steps.*

PROVERBS 16:9 NRSV

Your carefully-thought-through plans may not play out as you envisioned they would. Life isn't predictable. Certainly it's not perfect. But one thing is sure. God knows the way through the good and disappointing times. He guides your steps, bringing opportunities across your path that will shape your character and help you to become the wise woman you long to be. Let God direct you. He knows the way. He is the absolute best trail guide you could ever have.

*Lord, before I set out to do anything,*
*remind me to come to You. Let this become*
*a habit with me. You know the way, Lord.*

## Purposeful Living

*In all your ways acknowledge Him,*
*and He shall direct your paths.*

PROVERBS 3:6 NKJV

President Abraham Lincoln said that the good thing about the future is that it comes only one day at a time. That's a relief, because if you had to determine up front how you would live each moment of the rest of your life, you would be...well, massively overwhelmed! So right now ask God to direct you today. Tomorrow you can do it again. Your daily trust creates a lifetime of purposeful living.

*Help me to take things one day at a time, Father.*
*I'm only promised today. I don't want to expend energy*
*worrying about what might not happen tomorrow!*

# Light Bulbs

*The discerning heart seeks knowledge.*
PROVERBS 15:14 NIV

Some people confuse gullibility with open-mindedness. But think for a moment. Believing everything you're told could make you a target for unscrupulous people. God doesn't want you to be vulnerable to wrongdoers. When you seek His wisdom, He promises you a heart of discernment that creates a desire to study and discover the truth. That's when you will experience light bulbs of understanding lighting up your heart and mind.

*Jesus, I ask You to fill me with Your wisdom.*
*Plant discernment in my mind and heart as I make*
*choices and judgments about society and ideals.*

# Worth the Journey

*The wise in heart are called discerning,*
*and gracious words promote instruction.*

PROVERBS 16:21 NIV

Discernment is the ability to distinguish between the genuine and the counterfeit. It's the power to grasp what doesn't make sense. When you develop a discerning heart, you enjoy music, art, and godly things with deeper insight, although you recognize you'll never understand everything perfectly all the time. You become ready to share the joy with others—not in an "I got it. You need it" way, but with empathy and gentleness. It's a process worth the journey.

*Lord, please place a desire in me to see and love*
*others as You do. Fill my heart with joy and*
*gentleness as I live the life You've given me.*

## Disciplined Step

*To learn, you must love discipline.*

PROVERBS 12:1 NLT

Discipline. Sometimes this word summons memories of disapproving grade-school teachers. But discipline isn't really about scolding and pointing out flaws. It's about learning and enjoying life. Discipline is a good thing—and self-discipline multiplies the advantage. It allows you the privilege of taking responsibility for your own growth. Don't you love the thought of accomplishing your long-held physical, mental, relational, and spiritual dreams? This week, partner with God to take a disciplined step toward reaching one of your goals.

*Heavenly Father, I ask You to take fear out of the idea of "discipline" and to help me see it as something that draws me closer to Your will for me.*

# *Relax and Enjoy*

*"Mark a life of discipline and live wisely."*
PROVERBS 8:33 MSG

As a wise woman with a heart for God, you listen to instruction, consider your options, and then make intentional plans to practice what you've learned. You're focused, but not driven. You discover methods that help you exercise, sleep, and eat well. Allowing time for surprises and spontaneous service, you schedule your calendar sensibly. You're also gentle with yourself when you make inevitable human mistakes, because you know God wants you to relax and enjoy your life with Him.

*Father, I need lots of help scheduling my calendar*
*sensibly! I want to plan my days in healthy ways*
*so that I can live well and enjoy my life with You.*

# Resources and Knowledge

*Discretion will preserve you;*
*understanding will keep you.*

PROVERBS 2:11 NKJV

Sometimes when a farmer wants to protect his territory, he plants a thorny hedge around the perimeter. He hopes it will protect his land and possessions from harm.

Discretion—or the ability to meditate, think, purpose, and plan—works like a protective hedge in your life. Not only does God provide you with wisdom and instruction for making wise decisions, but He also helps you gain the resources and knowledge needed for reasoning, organizing, and implementing your future plans.

*Heavenly Father, I open my heart and mind*
*to all You want to pour into me. I ask for wisdom*
*and discernment as I follow Your plans for me.*

# Planning and Purposing

*As a ring of gold in a swine's snout,*
*so is a lovely woman who lacks discretion.*
PROVERBS 11:22 NKJV

For a little comic relief, picture a large, muddy sow with a shiny gold ring in her snout. Rather ridiculous, isn't it? And highly unlikely. It's just as ridiculous and unlikely for a beautiful woman of God—lovely from the inside out— to live her daily life without exercising discretion. It's just not going to happen. Although gaining wisdom is an ongoing process, be assured that as you grow, you'll learn practical skills for planning and purposing your life.

*Lord, I thank You for my personality. As I get older,*
*I ask You to enhance my personality and*
*character with more wisdom and discernment.*

# Empathize

*Singing cheerful songs to a person with a heavy heart is like taking someone's coat in cold weather or pouring vinegar in a wound.*

PROVERBS 25:20 NLT

Perhaps you've noticed how uncomfortable it feels to be with someone who just lost her job or broke up with her boyfriend. You want to help change her mood. But often the most helpful thing you can do is empathize. Listen. Agree that she hurts. Verify her disappointment. It allows her to accept herself so she can eventually move on—in her own time. This releases you from trying to come up with the perfect cheerful words to say.

*Father, forgive me for the times I try to fix others. Even when it seems that friends want or need fixing, that is not my job. Help me to give love and a listening ear instead.*

## Be Compassionate

*The person who shuns the bitter moments of
friends will be an outsider at their celebrations.*
PROVERBS 14:10 MSG

You can't predict what will happen next year or even one hour from now. Sometimes circumstances bring happy moments. Other times you get news that rocks your world. When you feel sad or mistreated, you'd rather someone empathize than discount your reality. If friends disregard your pain often enough, you'll probably hesitate to share much else with them, even your joy-filled times. God wants you and your friends to be compassionate with one another whether times are sad or happy.

*Lord, cultivate a firm foundation of truth in me so
that when friends share their "real" with me, I am
not shaken and can offer compassion instead.*

# A Richer Place

*The words of the godly encourage many.*
PROVERBS 10:21 NLT

Everyone needs encouragement. Your best friend needs it. Your son and daughter need it. Your pastor needs it. So does your sister. Your boss needs it. The deliveryman needs it. If you're married, your husband needs it—even though he may not act like he does. And what about you? Do you crave some encouragement today? It's okay to verbalize your desire, just as it's good to encourage others with your words. Mutual encouragement makes the world a richer place.

*Father, encourage me with Your love and truth as I start this day. Let Your encouragement to me carry over into everyone I come in contact with today.*

# Encouraging Words

*Wise words satisfy like a good meal.*
PROVERBS 18:20 NLT

Think of your favorite meal. It might be a white-tablecloth dinner of grilled salmon or steak. Or a casual setting with hamburger and french fries. Maybe vegetarian fare is your style. Whatever you prefer, it's a satisfying experience when you see, smell, and taste your favorite feast. Likewise, encouraging words of approval, support, gratitude, hope, and commendation—mixed with supportive actions—satisfy the soul. . .yours and the souls of your loved ones. How will you encourage someone today?

*Lord, let Your Word dwell in me richly like a fine meal. And as I share Your words with others, let it satisfy their soul in new ways.*

# Equality

*The rich and the poor shake hands
as equals—GOD made them both!*
PROVERBS 22:2 MSG

Intelligent men and women through the ages have insisted that all people are created equal. American leaders Thomas Jefferson, Elizabeth Cady Stanton, and Abraham Lincoln are a few. Yet long before they spoke about equality, the Bible included similar sentiments. God is the Creator of all human beings whether they are rich, poor, dark, light, quick, or slow. You have the right to breathe, think, act, and live freely—as does the woman living 1,000 miles from you.

*Heavenly Father, I know that You are no respecter of persons or positions. You see us all as Your children. Let me see others with Your eyes.*

## *Eyes to See*

*The poor and the oppressor have this in common:*
*the Lord gives light to the eyes of both.*

PROVERBS 29:13 NRSV

Someone once said, "You and I are equal with the human race. No better than. No less than." When we believe this, it changes our lives. We grow to work, play, love, and serve with greater love, patience, and acceptance. No person is on this earth to "lord it over" another. Neither is one here to be a doormat for someone else. As God does for each individual, He gives you eyes to see others as your equals.

*Lord, I pray that You would help me to live my*
*life to please You and not those that I view as*
*being better than me. Give me Your eyes to see.*

## More Than Precious Jewels

*A good woman is hard to find,*
*and worth far more than diamonds.*
PROVERBS 31:10 MSG

God created men and women with the capacity to reason, feel, choose, plan, and execute. After designing the first male and female and putting them in charge of His creation, He declared it all "very good." Yet sometimes women grade themselves by measurements other than God's, consequently setting unrealistic standards for themselves. Be gentle with yourself today. You're worth far more than precious jewels.

*Father, You created me specifically to be a*
*woman with a high calling. Clothe me with*
*Your armor and remind me of my true worth.*

# Only God

*Unrelenting disappointment leaves you heartsick,*
*but a sudden good break can turn life around.*
PROVERBS 13:12 MSG

I should. . ." "He must. . ." "I have to. . ." When your self-chatter repeatedly includes these phrases, you may believe the lie that people, projects, and circumstances have the ability to be perfect. Expecting perfection causes everyone and everything in your life to become a continual disappointment. It's better to accept the truth: people, actions, and situations don't have the ability to be constantly flawless on earth. Only God is perfect. Isn't that a relief?

*Lord, please forgive me for expecting perfection*
*out of my family. . .and myself. Change my heart*
*and fill me with grace for myself and others.*

## Not Alone

*Trust GOD from the bottom of your heart;*
*don't try to figure out everything on your own.*
PROVERBS 3:5 MSG

Doubts come. They're part of your inherent humanness. God knows that. Things have happened to you that make trusting Him seem foolish. It can feel like the ultimate paradox to release what you've worked so hard to cultivate. Yet God loves you and wants to ease your fear and anxiety. Picture this: unclenching the fist of your heart and releasing the problems you've tried relentlessly to figure out on your own. You don't have to do life alone. God waits patiently.

*Creator God, thank You for giving me the ability*
*to choose. Give me the desire to step out in faith*
*to choose and trust You with all that I am.*

# Letting Go

*Whoever trusts in the LORD will be enriched.*

PROVERBS 28:25 NRSV

What is faith, anyway? Is it the church you attend? The creed you follow? In part, but it's deeper than that. Faith involves confidence in God's ability to finish what He started in you, trusting He will do what you can't figure out. Personal faith means loosening your grip on your family, job, circumstances, and future. You let go, not into the unknown universe, but to your loving Father. And in this letting go you find freedom and life.

*I ask for Your very life to come and inhabit me, God.*
*Help my unbelief. Fill me with joy and freedom as*
*I release people and circumstances to Your care.*

## Warm and Safe

*The integrity of good people
creates a safe place for living.*
PROVERBS 14:32 MSG

Whatever your role—sister, aunt, mother, daughter, wife—you enjoy sharing good times with those you love. You also want them to feel comfortable approaching you with their disappointments. But how? A wise woman knows that others feel safe with someone who's the same on the inside as she is on the outside—one who listens first and then talks. Ask God to help you create a warm and safe place for your family to live and share.

*Lord, remove all pretense in me. Search my heart and show me anything that gets in the way of my authenticity. Let me be a safe and healthy person for Your daughters.*

## Invite God

*Old people are proud of their grandchildren,*
*and children are proud of their parents.*

PROVERBS 17:6 NCV

Families are God's idea. He created the concept of a loving unit—mother, father, and children—growing and learning together through challenges, disappointments, celebrations, moves, births, deaths, and surprises. There's no other group quite like the family. It has been said that you didn't choose your parents or your siblings, and it's true. But God is pleased when you support one another, relishing each other's gifts, dreams, and accomplishments with pride. Invite God to love your family through you.

*When family relationships are tough, Lord, please*
*help me to love them boldly. To speak truth in loving*
*ways and to share grace and mercy when needed.*

## *Fear of the Lord*

*The fear of the LORD is the beginning of wisdom.*
PROVERBS 9:10 NRSV

Fear blocks intimacy. It can hinder you from trying new things and cause you to obsess about finances or health. Fear threatens your contentment—even when you don't want it to. You want to be wise, free from fear. Then you read: "The fear of the Lord is the beginning of wisdom." Must you fear God too? Yet, to "fear" God means to respect and reverence Him with deepest adoration. When you do, everyday fear begins to fade and wisdom flourishes.

*Heavenly Father, I honor You in holiness. I respect Your great power and authority over all that is and has been made. I trust You with my life.*

## *Honor and Trust*

---

*Fear of the LORD is the foundation of true knowledge.*
PROVERBS 1:7 NLT

Building a house means making critical decisions about subcontractors, materials, design elements, and more. Ask any builder and you'll discover that constructing the foundation is one of the most important tasks, because if it's not properly laid, the entire edifice will be unstable. Likewise, as you develop a life of wisdom, you'll want to lay a strong foundation based on your faith in God. As you honor and trust Him, every area of your life will be built on this strength.

---

*Lord Jesus, place a desire in me to trust You with every decision. . .even the small ones. I know You care and want to give me counsel and wisdom in all things.*

## Finances

*Whoever makes deals with strangers is sure to get burned;*
*if you keep a cool head, you'll avoid rash bargains.*

PROVERBS 11:15 MSG

Whether the economy is good or bad, promises of easy success flash across your television screen, pop up during online searches, and arrive in both your email and snail-mail boxes. It's tempting to hop on board to get the best deal before it's too late. Yet God's wisdom instructs you to be thorough and check out the people behind the "good deals" before signing on. God wants to protect you financially.

*I'm so thankful for the guidebook You've given me, Lord.*
*You have offered wisdom for every situation I face. Help*
*me to access just what I need and to do what it says.*

## Enjoy What You Have

*Don't wear yourself out trying to get rich;*
*be wise enough to control yourself.*
PROVERBS 23:4 NCV

With your income, you probably buy groceries, pay your mortgage, clothe and educate your children, decorate your home, and give to others. When you don't have adequate finances, you feel the loss. Yet it's easy to try too hard to accumulate wealth. If you overwork, you'll neglect your health, loved ones, and God, and you'll end up exhausted. But you don't have to live this way. You can learn to balance your life, control your resources, and enjoy what you have.

*Lord, help me to be wise in my financial decisions.*
*Remind me to come to You before I make extra*
*purchases and overextend myself and my family.*

# Blessing-Filled Life

*Whoever walks with the wise becomes wise.*
PROVERBS 13:20 NRSV

Isn't it amazing how diverse friendships can be? You may have friends for different seasons of your life or friends with whom you share a particular interest, friends you've had forever, and friends you've just met. It's essential, though, that you include those who are wise in your circle of friends. Spending time with people who have sound judgment will help you stay clear-headed and moving in the direction of a blessing-filled life.

*Thank You for friendships, Lord! I ask that You place several friends in my life who are wise and deeply in love with You. . .to walk alongside me and give good counsel.*

# Thankful

*A friend loves at all times.*
PROVERBS 17:17 NRSV

Having a loving friend makes you feel rich even when you don't have this month's rent money. When your child gets picked up by the police, a true friend hangs in there with you. She cries when your mother dies—and stays in touch when you move away. A loyal friend's hug reassures you that your public blunder wasn't the end of the world. Today, thank a friend for her constant love.

*I am blessed by good friendships, Father God. Help me to be a loyal friend to those You've placed in my life. Let our friendship be filled with freedom, love, truth, and life.*

## Tomorrow

*Always respect the Lord.*
*Then you will have hope for the future.*
PROVERBS 23:17–18 NCV

Even for wise women of God, the future sometimes appears blurry. What do you do when circumstances change? Plans don't work out like you thought they would? You lose something you cherish? There are no cookie-cutter answers. Yet as a woman with a heart for God, you can pause and remember when God has helped you in the past. You might even write these memories down. Now choose to let these previous times give you hope for what you'll face tomorrow.

*Thank You for the bumps along the way, Lord. I can go back and see how You were close to me and how You worked in my life. Thank You for Your faithfulness.*

## Hope for the Future

*The drippings of the honeycomb are sweet
to your taste. Know that wisdom is such to
your soul; if you find it, you will find a future.*

PROVERBS 24:13–14 NRSV

Some experts say that honey is a miracle food. It rarely spoils, contains no fat or cholesterol, and helps burn fats while you sleep. Yet it's most known for sweetness. Even thinking about honey-drizzled desserts makes your taste buds salivate in anticipation. Like honey is to your taste, wisdom—that unique understanding, knowledge, and insight about all the various aspects of life—is to your soul. No wonder gaining God's wisdom gives you hope for the future.

*Fill me with Your wisdom and truth, Lord God.
Give me the desire to be in Your Word, and let the
Holy Spirit make Your Word come alive in me.*

# Generosity

*A quietly given gift soothes an irritable person;*
*a heartfelt present cools a hot temper.*
PROVERBS 21:14 MSG

A knee-jerk reaction to an irritable clerk is to snap back. When a friend shoots an angry remark your direction, you may want to retaliate. However, when you offer the gift of a quiet response or understanding word, your generous act can defuse the tension. Even a gift of time or money can make a positive difference. Offer homemade cookies, a lunch out, to take out the trash, or to help with another project. Your quietly given gift can cool a heated situation.

*Lord Jesus, I want to be a more generous person. . .*
*with gifts, time, patience, and mercy. Give me*
*wisdom to know what gifts to offer and when.*

## Worlds Expand

*The world of the generous gets larger and larger.*
PROVERBS 11:24 MSG

Stories about celebrities' lifestyles splash across the magazine covers at grocery checkouts. Television news shows and internet sites follow their daily behavior and activities. Some make positive contributions to society. But you don't have to be a well-paid star to be generous. Success isn't calculated by dollars—it's calculated by who you are and what you willingly contribute. Your inner and outer worlds expand when you give generously from your personal storehouse.

*Make giving a priority in my life, Lord.*
*Whisper to me where and when I should*
*share with those in need around me.*

## Lovely Thought

*A woman of gentle grace gets respect.*
PROVERBS 11:16 MSG

Perhaps you've heard your local news reporter deliver Friday night's weather report and mention that the forecast includes balmy temperatures and gentle breezes. "So go outside and enjoy your weekend," she might add. Technically, a gentle breeze means a wind with a speed of eight to twelve miles per hour. Just enough to refresh without blowing things around. Now imagine gracefully traveling through your days at the speed of a gentle breeze, showing gentleness to yourself and others. Lovely thought, isn't it?

*Lord, please help me to be gentle with myself and others. Fill me with Your grace and allow that to spill over onto those around me.*

## Room for Peace

*A gentle answer turns away wrath.*
PROVERBS 15:1 NIV

God invites you to come to Him with your daily irritations and angst. He's not threatening you with ultimatums or put-downs if you don't. Instead He waits and promises to listen even when you're mad at yourself for falling off your diet or yelling at your kids or not making your deadline at work. May His gentleness encourage you to practice patience with yourself and others, thereby silencing the anger bully and making room for peace.

*God, I invite You into all my thoughts and feelings. I bring my anger and hurt feelings to You. Help me to sort them out with You so I don't act out in inappropriate ways.*

# Partner with God

*GOD's blessing makes life rich;*
*nothing we do can improve on God.*
PROVERBS 10:22 MSG

God is always the same, yet never boring. He's continuously good, creative, kind, compassionate, and timely. He protects, loves, and guides you, your family, your neighbors, your pastor, and those missionary friends twelve flight hours away. Every morning He's right beside you. He never walks out when you're talking to Him. Nothing you do can make God any better than He is. He rules the universe but knows what you're planning at 4:00 p.m. tomorrow. For exciting life adventures, partner with Him.

*Father, it is beyond my understanding how You created*
*all and yet know me intimately. I praise You for who*
*You are. Thank You for knowing and caring about me.*

## Inside and Out

*GOD is in charge of human life,*
*watching and examining us inside and out.*
PROVERBS 20:27 MSG

Pop stars sing tunes that bemoan how lovers and friends don't take time to really know one another. We hear lyrics similar to "He only talks about himself. . . ," "She left before we bonded. . . ," "He doesn't really know me. . . ."

People desire intimacy. So if you're like most folks, you want your loved ones to ask about your dreams, listen, and love you in spite of and because of what they hear. God does. He delights in knowing you inside and out.

*Lord, Your Word says that You search me*
*and know me. I open up my heart to You,*
*Lord. I want Your life to grow and move in me.*

## His Goodness

*So you may walk in the way of goodness. . .*
PROVERBS 2:20 NKJV

Archbishop Desmond Tutu, a Nobel Peace Prize recipient from South Africa, said, "The world is hungry for goodness." With so much immorality, power-mongering, and terrorism in the world, people long for the good. But what does that mean? Goodness is a basket full of rich characteristics that include excellence, virtue, beauty, joy, kindness, and wisdom. Genuine goodness counteracts moral evil. Sounds like a partial definition of God, doesn't it? Ask God to help you share His goodness with your world.

*Lord, I desire Your goodness. Not only in my actions but also that my heart would be good on the inside. Set my heart on You, and allow me to walk in Your ways.*

# Reflect God's Grace

*Your generosity will surprise him with goodness,*
*and GOD will look after you.*

PROVERBS 25:22 MSG

H eap coals of fire upon his head." You've probably heard this line before. It originated from the wisest man who ever lived. "If your enemy is hungry, give him food to eat; if he is thirsty, give him water to drink," wrote King Solomon. "In doing this, you will heap burning coals on his head." It's opposite of how you might want to treat a stubborn foe. Yet your generous response will shock him with goodness and reflect God's grace.

*Father, help me to respond to unkindness with grace.*
*Let me think first before bursting out with angry retorts.*
*Help me to reflect Your goodness and grace.*

# *Exhale of Grace*

---

*Keep sound wisdom and discretion; so they*
*will be life to your soul and grace to your neck.*
PROVERBS 3:21–22 NKJV

Would you like to be less self-critical? Reduce the silent inner nit-picking? It's possible, and it happens as you develop wisdom, discretion, and grace in the midst of your humanness. As you accept God's unmerited love through His Son, Jesus, realize that He grants you extra time to learn and grow and that He genuinely cares about your emotional, spiritual, and physical needs. Breathing in God's grace allows you to exhale that same grace onto others.

---

*Thank You for Your great love and amazing grace,*
*Lord God. You see me as righteous through Christ.*
*Grant me grace and peace as I learn Your ways.*

## Contagious Blessing

*A mean person gets paid back in
meanness, a gracious person in grace.*

PROVERBS 14:14 MSG

As you become a grace-full person, the judgmental, overachieving, demanding attitudes will shrink. You'll notice you're breathing deeply, enjoying life, and feeling more grateful and generous—not perfectly 24-7 (you're still human!), but increasingly. You won't suddenly be the ultimate expert on grace, yet you'll desire more—for yourself, your loved ones, and those you hardly know. When you enjoy being gracious at home, at work, and everywhere you go, it comes back to you like a contagious blessing.

*Let the love I receive from You be contagious, Lord.
Place a smile on my face and peace in my heart
that comes from knowing You. Thank You, Father.*

## Gratitude

---

*Ears to hear and eyes to see—*
*both are gifts from the L*ORD*.*
PROVERBS 20:12 NLT

Everything you have is a gift from God: the air you breathe, the sunset you enjoy, the rain that nourishes your garden, your work, love of family and friends, your taste buds, freedom, music, a bird's song, art, the creativity to design. All things are God's, and He shares them with you, to bring you pleasure. What are you grateful for today? Pause for a moment and thank Him for all His gifts.

---

*Lord, I am so grateful for all of the everyday blessings*
*You've given me! My friends, my family, my home...the*
*ability to see and read and enjoy creation. Thanks, God!*

## Change of Focus

*Honor God with everything you own; give him
the first and the best. Your barns will burst.*

PROVERBS 3:9–10 MSG

You make a wise choice when you honor God with your wealth—whether it is great wealth (by society's standards) or only a little. God blesses you when you share what you have. Forget about the idea that you need to overwork, overdo, and keep it up 24-7 in order to please God. That's your inner bully speaking and not our heavenly Father. Silence the inner tyrant by naming what you're thankful for. Gratitude changes your focus.

*Father God, please place a desire in my heart to be with
You and praise You before I start my day. I want my
focus to be on blessings rather than problems.*

## Daily Adventure

*The LORD gives wisdom; from his mouth come knowledge
and understanding; he stores up sound wisdom for the
upright; he is a shield to those who walk in integrity.*

PROVERBS 2:6–7 ESV

God is not stingy. He willingly and liberally shares His love, patience, instruction, and wisdom with you. Identify a characteristic or attribute you want to cultivate, and share your desire with God and another trustworthy person. Ask God to help you clarify your next step and then seek to learn as much as you can about it. God wants to be your guide on this daily adventure of learning, changing, and growing.

*You are the source of wisdom, Lord God. I ask that
You show me Your will for me, day by day. Give me
the courage to take the steps You ask of me.*

## Set Free to Grow

*The wise are mightier than the strong, and those with knowledge grow stronger and stronger.*

PROVERBS 24:5 NLT

King Solomon, author of most of the pithy sayings in Proverbs, didn't write a handbook for success, but an instruction manual for living a wise and meaningful life. No matter what the level of your academic education, you can be a knowledgeable, disciplined, perceptive, and discerning woman. When you understand that it is your choice how you live—and you decide to trust God—then you are set free to grow and become who God designed you to be.

*Thank You for setting me free, Jesus!*
*I invite You to do in me all that You intend.*
*Soften my heart as You work in me.*

# Half Full

*A cheerful look brings joy to the heart;*
*good news makes for good health.*
PROVERBS 15:30 NLT

Medical experts indicate that it does matter whether you see the proverbial glass half empty or half full. Many believe that positive thinking leads to lower rates of depression, increased life span, and reduced risk of death from heart disease. Consequently, health professionals urge their patients to cultivate optimistic attitudes. Guess what? God recommends this also. Search for the good news in your life today. Make a list and display it where you'll see it often.

*I ask You to change my heart and mind, Lord.*
*When things look dark and difficult, change my*
*thinking to see the good, positive things You can do.*

## Healing Can Begin

*A reliable messenger brings healing.*
PROVERBS 13:17 NLT

Just because you look for the good side of your circumstances doesn't mean that you deny reality. Sometimes problems exist that are impossible to ignore. To continue looking the other way is foolish. It's not wise or healthy to ignore addiction, abuse, signs of depression, or unpleasant medical symptoms. When a reliable person speaks up courageously, healing can begin. Maybe that person is you.

*Lord, please give me the courage to be honest about my inner life. . .with You and with safe people who can offer wisdom. I open my heart to Your healing.*

## Heartfelt

*Tune your ears to wisdom, and concentrate
on understanding. Cry out for insight,
and ask for understanding.*

PROVERBS 2:2–3 NLT

Past generations seemed to emphasize the non-emotional life approach. If you could see something with your physical eyes, prove it through scientific research, or touch it with your hands, it was considered valid. Recently there's been a shift to the "spiritual" side of human existence. But through it all, God hasn't changed. He's always cared about your heart and your intellect. Turn your thoughts and emotions over to God, asking Him for the understanding to make wise, heartfelt decisions in your everyday circumstances.

*Lord, You created me physically and emotionally.
This was Your idea. I trust You with my feelings,
and I ask that You become Lord over them.*

# Great News

*Trust in the LORD with all your heart.*
PROVERBS 3:5 NKJV

Singing about God in church, saying mealtime grace, attending Sunday school, and giving generously to the poor are worthwhile, God-honoring activities. Yet these good behaviors will never replace a genuine relationship with God. He longs to interact with you on a personal level. That's why God went to the trouble of sending His Son Jesus to earth to give His life for you. When you trust God wholeheartedly, nothing stands between you and Him. Isn't that great news?

*I want to trust You more, Jesus. I've seen what You can do! I believe You are who You say You are. I'm so thankful that You want to be in relationship with me.*

## Personal Privilege

*Do not withhold good from those to whom it is due,*
*when it is in the power of your hand to do so.*
PROVERBS 3:27 NKJV

The Bible provides a great basis for Sunday sermons about God and His plans. Yet it also includes nitty-gritty advice about acquiring people skills and cultivating a habit of bigheartedness. You can't assist everyone in this hurting world, but you can help in everyday ways—perhaps by carrying an elderly friend's heavy package, allowing a waiting driver into your lane, sharing pro bono business advice, or comforting a crying child. Helping is your personal privilege—and it's doable.

*Lord, I continue to ask that You open my eyes to see the problems around me and the ways that You have equipped me to help. Please help me do what needs to be done.*

## *Step Up*

---

*Rescue the perishing;*
*don't hesitate to step in and help.*
PROVERBS 24:11 MSG

When you reach out to pray, support, and act on behalf of those who cannot help themselves, you reflect God's loving concern for all people. However, walking beyond your own comfort to advocate for those suffering injustice, abuse, or inadequacy is not always easy. When do you step in? How do you help? You can't do it all. Yet you can ask God for direction and then step up courageously as He touches your heart with someone's need.

---

*I ask for courage again, Lord. I know what needs*
*to be done, but sometimes I lack the courage*
*to do it. Nudge me to do the right thing.*

# Home

*Through wisdom a house is built, and by understanding*
*it is established; by knowledge the rooms are filled*
*with all precious and pleasant riches.*

PROVERBS 24:3-4 NKJV

Perhaps you're frustrated that your home isn't like you pictured it would be. Your husband and children didn't turn out as you dreamed they would. Disappointment tugs at you. But nothing and no one is perfect here on this earth. Your loved ones have good and bad days, just like you do. That's okay, because if your home and family were flawless, you wouldn't need God. Trusting and gaining His understanding fills your heart and home with joy, love, and acceptance.

*Cultivate joy, love, and acceptance in me,*
*Father God. I want to offer the hope and grace*
*You offer me to my family, friends, and neighbors.*

## *Unique Job*

*A wise woman strengthens her family.*
PROVERBS 14:1 NCV

Maybe you can't wield a sledgehammer all afternoon. Perhaps you can't win the marathon year after year. Maybe you don't have stamina to sing oratorios or write annual bestselling books. But you are strong. As you seek God's wisdom, knowledge, and discernment, your inner strength increases. That's great news, because you've been given a unique job: the privilege of building and strengthening your home. Whether you have a family of one, two, five, or ten, God partners with you.

*Your calling on my life is great, Lord. I know this.*
*You have equipped me more than adequately*
*to hear from You and walk in Your ways.*

# Honesty

*The LORD wants honest balances and scales.*
PROVERBS 16:11 NCV

God values truth-telling. Years ago people used stone weights on scales to determine the measurements of the products they sold. Dishonest store owners labeled the stones incorrectly to pad their profits. Dishonesty saddened God then as it does now. God loves for His children to be honest. Yet sometimes it seems more comfortable to avoid the truth if it isn't to your advantage. Being honest with your personal and professional dealings and relationships takes God-given courage—and it's incredibly freeing.

*I want to be truthful with You, myself, and others, Father God. Cultivate integrity in my deepest parts. Help me to share truth and love with those around me.*

# Under Control

*Honest people are relaxed*
*and confident, bold as lions.*
PROVERBS 28:1 MSG

Throughout history, women have been admired for their strength, courage, and confidence. Jesus' mother, Mary, is no exception. Although she was a teenager and no doubt surprised when God called her to carry His Son, Jesus, she remained honest when it might have been easier to evade the truth. God calls you to be honest in your current circumstances too. And in that honesty, you'll find strength as you trust that God has it all under control.

*Help me to act honestly, Lord, despite any*
*consequences that may bring me. Give me*
*wisdom as I speak truth in every area of my life.*

## *Release and Relax!*

*Don't assume that you know it all.*
*Run to GOD!... Your body will glow with*
*health, your very bones will vibrate with life!*
PROVERBS 3:7–8 MSG

It's unrealistic to think you can figure out everything and everyone—even though you're a capable woman and some say you have eyes in the back of your head! Seriously, it's just too much pressure to try to know it all month after month, year after year. The stress takes a toll on your health. So as a woman committed to making wise choices, you can release your need to know, turn your concerns over to God, and relax.

*Oh Father, I definitely need to relax more!*
*Forgive me for trying to know everything and control*
*things I have no business controlling. Help me to let go!*

# Back to Grace

*He. . .shows favor to the humble.*

PROVERBS 3:34 NIV

We love grace. It represents kindness, favor, and beauty. Who doesn't want these pleasant gifts? But humility? It's difficult to understand and tougher still to desire. Yet God says He honors humility. In part, this means seeing yourself as God sees you: imperfect and needy, but forgiven and freed from what weighs you down through the death of Jesus on the cross. You recognize that God is God and you are not, and this acknowledgment brings you back to grace.

*My righteousness is in You alone, Lord Jesus.*
*I know that without You I'm an imperfect mess.*
*I'm so thankful that I am forgiven and free to be me.*

## Heart Actions

*GOD. . .relishes integrity.*
PROVERBS 11:20 MSG

God cares about integrity. He wants you to be the same inside as you appear outside. Some may think this integrity dilemma only shows up when someone pretends to love God but really doesn't. But there's a painful flip side that women encounter when they deeply desire God but live to please someone else instead. Thankfully, there's a cure. Courageously permit your heart to influence your actions, even when it's uncomfortable. God will help.

*Father God, forgive me for the times I've set someone else in Your place. Remove any and all idols I have in my life. You alone deserve that space in my heart.*

## Heart of Integrity

*A hot furnace tests silver and gold,*
*but the LORD tests hearts.*
PROVERBS 17:3 NCV

"Lord, show me who I am now and who I can become—the woman You had in mind when You created me." With this prayer, you begin the lifelong process of becoming you—learning your passions, gifts, talents, and God-given personality. You start to discover what holds you back and what you need to move forward. It starts in the heart. God investigates your heart and shares His findings with you. Together you create a heart of integrity.

*Father God, I invite You in to show me who I am and*
*the ways You want to work in me as I live this life.*
*Show me where I'm stuck and how to move forward.*

# Act with Intentionality

*She looks over a field and buys it, then,*
*with money she's put aside, plants a garden.*
PROVERBS 31:16 MSG

You've heard it before: Be proactive. But what does it mean? In part it means to initiate wise change instead of merely reacting to problems. For example, you set a goal to eat healthier. You pray about it, make a plan, research options, and visualize the outcome. But that's not enough. You need to act on your plan to see it come to fruition. You and your goals are important to God. Ask Him to help you act intentionally.

*Lord, lay out goals for me that align with*
*Your will. Then help me to be intentional*
*as I act on what You've shown me.*

# Aren't You Glad?

*It's the child he loves that GOD corrects;*
*a father's delight is behind all this.*
PROVERBS 3:12 MSG

God delights in coaching you toward maturity. Just as a caring, patient human father does, He enjoys showing you new adventures, planning methods to help you learn, and watching you practice and gain confidence in your new skills. When He notices that you need direction, He corrects you—similar to what an earthly father does when he sees his child throw the softball improperly. God is intentional about training and encouraging you. Aren't you glad He loves you like that?

*Heavenly Father, You are the best dad! You are good*
*and perfect. You parent me completely and lovingly.*
*I'm so thankful for Your direction and wisdom.*

## A Little Joy

*Those who promote peace have joy.*
PROVERBS 12:20 NIV

Doesn't it seem like someone is always promoting something? A new book. An updated diet. A time-management program. An insurance policy. A charity opportunity. A miracle medicine. A new money-making system. The latest powerful vacuum cleaner. Any or all of these ideas may have merit. Yet for those who promote peace, harmony, well-being, and fulfillment, there's certain joy. God delights in you, and you are privileged to share that delight-filled encouragement with others. Go ahead. Market a little joy today.

*In a world where everyone seems to be selling something,*
*I ask that You help me to offer something free: joy that*
*comes from knowing You personally, Jesus!*

# Genuine Joy

*The hope of the righteous brings joy.*

PROVERBS 10:28 ESV

There's an ongoing debate rumbling around: What's the difference between a Christian and a nonbeliever? Even those who don't follow Christ often agree the difference is hope—the sure expectation that God is on your side and you'll spend eternity with Him, no matter what happens during your earthly life. Beyond all the good deeds you can muster, you're made righteous in God's eyes by the gift of Christ's life, death, and resurrection. And that hope brings genuine joy.

*Lord, Your Word tells me that You abide in me! You are my living hope. I don't have to wait for the afterlife to experience Your Presence. You are with me now.*

# *Justice*

*Speak up for those who cannot speak for themselves;
ensure justice for those being crushed.*

PROVERBS 31:8 NLT

When good people keep silent, injustice and abuse prevail. Remember the well-planned Nazi extermination of the Jews before World War II? Think of the many news stories detailing the tragic deaths of innocent children at the hands of their abusive parents. Results would be different if someone had successfully interceded. If you find it daunting to challenge bullies, you're not alone. It is intimidating. But may godly people everywhere join together and ask God for courage to follow His directive.

*You have planted a sense of justice in my heart, Lord.
Use that for Your purposes. Show me what I can
do to help, and give me courage to do it.*

## Speak Up

*Yes, speak up for the poor and helpless,*
*and see that they get justice.*

PROVERBS 31:9 NLT

God cares about the disadvantaged, the mistreated, the persecuted, and the mocked; children who go hungry; abused spouses; pastors who get thrown in jail for preaching from the Bible; and Christian university students who become targets of intolerance and prejudice. God asks us to speak out in the midst of injustice. Yet you may wonder if your single voice matters. It does. Join with other godly voices to send a message that can't be dismissed.

*I'm thankful for the voice You've given me, Lord.*
*Help me to be wise when I use it. Give me courage*
*as I speak up when my voice is needed.*

# Loving-Kindness

*What is desired. . .is kindness.*
PROVERBS 19:22 NKJV

Have you noticed that kindness sometimes seems like a lost commodity? It's understandable. Everyone's in such a hurry and on alert 24-7. You hear recorded messages when you call for an important appointment. When you need help on the highway, it's often "tough luck." Then someone graces you with a spontaneous act of kindness and your mood brightens. God knew that would happen. It's His plan. He treats you with loving-kindness, so you can share it with others.

*Your Word tells me that it's Your loving-kindness
that draws us to repentance, Lord. Let me love
others well out of Your great kindness to me.*

## Extra Kindness

*She opens her mouth with wisdom,*
*and the teaching of kindness is on her tongue.*
PROVERBS 31:26 NRSV

No matter what your season of life, you are influencing someone. In your job you may train others or greet clients on the phone or have lunch with coworkers. At home you interact with neighbors, your parents, your husband, and your child. At church you may teach a class or sing in the choir. Perhaps you deal with teachers at school or live with peers in a retirement community. Whatever your interactions this week, add a little extra kindness.

*Lord, remind me that every interaction I have with*
*another person can leave them with a smile or a frown.*
*Help me to spread Your love and kindness around.*

# Doing Right

*Pay attention to my wisdom, turn your ear to
my words of insight, that you may maintain
discretion and your lips may preserve knowledge.*

PROVERBS 5:1-2 NIV

If you're somewhat confused about the difference between wisdom and knowledge, you're not alone. Many women doubt they'll ever be truly wise (or successful) because they don't have the credentials that others do. Sometimes they retreat and miss the rewards of living as the women God created them to be. Knowledge accumulates information—and that's valuable. Wisdom combines your heart knowledge, experience, and gifts, then moves past knowing to doing what is right—and that's possible when you partner with God.

*God, fill me with Your kind of wisdom. Let the
hearts of others matter more to me than knowledge.*

## Seeking Wisdom

*For giving prudence to those who are simple, knowledge*
*and discretion to the young—let the wise listen and add*
*to their learning, and let the discerning get guidance.*
PROVERBS 1:4–5 NIV

God loves helping you grow wise. He also loves seeing you learn new things and adding to your inner pool of knowledge. The more discerning you become, the more you are able to help others who need understanding and wisdom to make important choices that will impact their lives. God loves you so much, and He is pleased with you for seeking to be a wiser and more knowledgeable woman, a woman He can use to bless others.

*I ask that You teach me Your Word, Lord God,*
*so that I might know and understand people*
*and circumstances better through Your eyes.*

## Opportunity for Laughter

*A cheerful heart is a good medicine.*
PROVERBS 17:22 NRSV

The world is filled with trouble, stress, and responsibility. It can be pretty tough at times to keep your sense of humor and your positive perspective. Laughter breaks the tension and allows your body and soul to take a deep, healing breath. It lifts you up when everything around you is pulling you down. No matter what your circumstances, look for opportunities to laugh, and if you don't find any, create some of your own.

*Thank You for the great gift of laughter,*
*heavenly Father. It is good for my body, mind,*
*and spirit. Allow it to bubble up in me more.*

## A Happy Heart

*A glad heart makes a cheerful countenance.*
PROVERBS 15:13 NRSV

Grab the latest women's magazines from the rack at your local grocery checkout. After browsing the articles and ads, you may notice that their brand of beauty comes from wearing this season's lip gloss shades, lengthening your eyelashes, finding the perfect blush, and concealing all age spots. The products that promise all this may make you look more polished, but your entire expression changes when you have a happy heart—one that easily gives way to smiles, gratitude, and laughter.

*Fill my heart with gladness, Lord.*
*Let my face shine from a heart full of*
*love and joy that is found in You alone.*

# Leading Well

*Good leadership is a channel of water controlled by GOD; he directs it to whatever ends he chooses.*

PROVERBS 21:1 MSG

Y ou are a leader. Maybe you don't think so, but you are. Someone looks up to you and would like your support, advice, and encouragement. Perhaps you doubt your ability to lead well. Still, you long to live and inspire others with a sincere heart—with intentionality, wisdom, and grace. Be encouraged, because God loves to guide you. Partner with Him, and be assured that He's working in you to influence others for good.

*Thank You for coming alongside me in this leadership journey, Lord. I feel incapable at times. Remind me that You are my guide.*

# A Transformed Heart

*Love and truth form a good leader;*
*sound leadership is founded on loving integrity.*

PROVERBS 20:28 MSG

Intentional leaders work at becoming proactive in life and ministry. But perhaps you wonder what it means to be purposeful or intentional. Being unintentional is being haphazard about your personal and spiritual growth and your ministry deeds—merely reacting to whatever need comes along. You'll find fulfillment in your leadership roles when you seek God's wise direction about your unique gifting, serving with integrity and loving with a transformed heart.

*Jesus, I want to lead by Your example. Help me*
*to be intentional about my time with You and*
*the leadership opportunities You've given me.*

# A Legacy

*The Fear-of-God builds up confidence,*
*and makes a world safe for your children.*

PROVERBS 14:26 MSG

"The family that prays together stays together." You may have heard—and believed—this adage. You take your children to church and encourage them to listen to their teachers and to follow God's directives. That's good, but the greatest thing you can do for them is to face your own wrong before God, accept Jesus as God's provision for your need, and grow spiritually. As they see you trust God, it will inspire them to do the same.

*Lord, I desire to leave a strong legacy for my*
*children. Let them see me live a transformed*
*life that honors You in all I think, say, and do.*

# Beyond Earthly Years

*The godly walk with integrity;*
*blessed are their children who follow them.*
PROVERBS 20:7 NLT

You probably want your children to have what you didn't have growing up, to learn what you didn't learn, to experience what you didn't experience, and to make wise choices. So you correct their behavior and help them learn to solve their own problems. Although telling them to be honest and good is important, showing and modeling integrity and transformation is key. Your loving acceptance and example will bless them and leave a rich legacy that lasts far beyond your earthly years.

*Creator God, help me to accept the imperfections*
*of my children. Let me love them through it*
*and model integrity and grace as I parent.*

# Fresh Meaning

*The Fear-of-GOD expands your life.*
PROVERBS 10:27 MSG

People seem hungry for something to give their lives meaning. If you listen to current hit songs, you'd think that meaning comes from having another human being love you more than anyone else in the world. But what happens when that love interest gets mad, disappoints you, or finds someone else? Life becomes a drag. Only developing a relationship with God through Jesus Christ will fill that hole in your heart. Let Him give your life fresh meaning.

*Open my eyes and heart to hear from You,*
*Lord Jesus. You alone are the One who can*
*bring me life and make my heart whole.*

# New Life

*Respect for the LORD gives life. It is like a*
*fountain that can save people from death.*

PROVERBS 14:27 NCV

The more you grow to respect God, the more you appreciate His daily gifts and enjoy being with Him. Maybe you pause more often to ask Him for His advice. You know your life is richer now (and will be for eternity) because you believe that Jesus, God's Son, gave His life for you. Even though you don't understand it all, you feel like there's a fresh stream of water flowing through your heart, giving you new life.

*Lord, please remove any rubble and rocks that may*
*prevent Your streams of living water from flowing*
*through me. I invite You in to wash me anew.*

## Mutual Growth

*Spouting off before listening to the
facts is both shameful and foolish.*
PROVERBS 18:13 NLT

How do you feel when someone listens to you without telling you what to do? Research indicates that this type of interaction helps people find their own answers and take intentional action. Most women (men and children too) long to be heard and understood. Yet it's difficult to hear another's bewilderment, pain, or joy when you interject your own thoughts and opinions. You may long to provide solutions, but it's wise to listen to the whole story before giving advice. Listening encourages mutual growth.

*Father God, forgive me for the times I've wanted my own voice to be heard instead of listening to a friend's struggle. Give me wisdom as I listen and share as You prompt me.*

## Rich Insights

*Wise men and women are always learning,*
*always listening for fresh insights.*
PROVERBS 18:15 MSG

Listening offers a win-win scenario for relationships—at home, work, church, or in the neighborhood. However, it's common to sometimes focus on the chatter in your own head while another person is talking. A wise woman learns to concentrate on the other person and listen for the message and reality beneath the content of a person's words. When you listen on a deeper level, you gain rich insights about life, others, yourself, and God.

*Lord, I really need help to become a better*
*listener. Give me Your love for each person*
*who is speaking and needing a listening ear.*

# Marriage

*Let your wife be a fountain of blessing for you.*
*Rejoice in the wife of your youth.*

PROVERBS 5:18 NLT

Marriage involves two people—a man and a woman. You both share responsibility for the success, happiness, and godliness of your union. As a wise woman, you can't make a man love and honor you. Neither will a wise man demand you to love and respect him. Wisdom recommends that as husband and wife, you cherish one another, finding blessing in each other above all others, remaining sexually and emotionally faithful throughout your lives together.

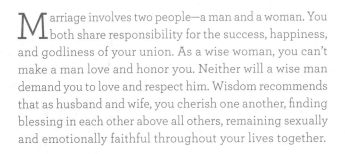

*Father God, I ask for Your blessing on our marriage.*
*Let us mutually submit to one another out of love,*
*just as we submit our lives to You.*

## Joy That Is Contagious

*A virtuous and capable wife. . .is more precious than rubies. Her husband can trust her, and she will greatly enrich his life. She brings him good, not harm.*

PROVERBS 31:10–12 NLT

If you're a wife, God wants you to appreciate the good things your husband does for you, your family, and your friends. God desires that you value your husband's ideas and that he values yours. As a committed follower of Christ, you don't live through your husband, but with him. You wisely allow your husband to take responsibility for his own decisions and growth; thus he trusts you. As you work together, you both experience a joy that is contagious.

*Lord, I ask that You fill our marriage with a joy that we've not known before. Surprise us with Your goodness in marriage. Let our love shine for You.*

## *Mercy*

---

*Guilt is banished through love and truth.*
PROVERBS 16:6 MSG

We have a problem. You can sense it when you try to be good and can't—at least not for long. You can feel it when patience eludes you. Sometimes you panic as fear threatens your fledgling faith. Consequently you know. We know. God is perfect; we aren't. But God banishes the weight of our guilt with His love exhibited in Jesus, who said, "I am the Truth." Then you believe and are free.

---

*I cannot begin to understand Your great love*
*for me, Jesus! But I trust that it's true, and I*
*choose to live in freedom and grace because of it!*

129

## Blessed Relief

*You can't whitewash your sins and get by with it;*
*you find mercy by admitting and leaving them.*

PROVERBS 28:13 MSG

Have you ever wondered what sin includes? Some say you sin when you don't act in the way they believe you should, or when you fail to go to church several times a week. Yet God says sin is living like He doesn't matter. We can't pretend we haven't treated God this way at times. It's the human predicament. So you can stop trying to be what you aren't, admit your need, and find mercy. Now isn't that blessed relief?

*Help me to stop running from my sins and failures, Lord.*
*I'm done with that. I ask that You open my heart today*
*and begin the rebuilding process of making me new.*

## Wisdom and Discernment

*Better is a dry morsel with quiet than
a house full of feasting with strife.*
PROVERBS 17:1 NRSV

Spending money allows you to make positive differences at home, in your city, and the world. You can provide opportunities for education, enhance enjoyment of the arts, build beautiful homes, feed hungry children, and fund worthwhile projects. In your personal life, money helps you to pay rent, buy groceries, heat your home, provide your children with music lessons, and secure health coverage. Yet money doesn't buy harmony, tranquility, or unity. First seek wisdom and then spend with discernment.

*Everything You've given me is a gift, Lord. Remind me
of that always. Help me to be generous and make
wise choices with the gifts You've given me.*

## Stand Secure

*A thick bankroll is no help when life falls apart,*
*but a principled life can stand up to the worst.*
PROVERBS 11:4 MSG

How much does she make? Where does he live? What are they worth? Perhaps you've heard questions like these. Our culture values money and those who accumulate it. People who have "made it financially" hold great influence. It's understandable, for money can do a lot. Yet a thick bankroll doesn't guarantee emotional, mental, or spiritual strength when trouble comes. Your wise life with God will stand secure when money lets you down. And with that you can rest easier.

*I put my faith in You alone, Lord God.*
*Money provides a false sense of security,*
*but I know that You are the only sure foundation.*

## All God's

*"God stretched out Earth's Horizons,
and tended to the minute details of Soil
and Weather, and set Sky firmly in place."*

PROVERBS 8:26-27 MSG

Picture yourself standing on a cliff gazing down on the crashing waves. Close your eyes and imagine walking in the mountains among the tall trees. Can you smell the pine? Hear the wind through the leaves? Now, close this book, go outside, and stare at the sky. Blue? Cloudy? Rainy? Whatever you find, it's all God's. All this loveliness is the work of His hands. He created it for His glory and your delight. So go and enjoy!

*Thank You for the gift of Your creation,
heavenly Father! What an amazing picture
of Your love and creativity. I praise You, God!*

## God-Designed

*I'll never understand—how an eagle flies*
*so high in the sky, how a snake glides over*
*a rock, how a ship navigates the ocean.*
PROVERBS 30:18-19 MSG

Have you ever watched a documentary on birds, reptiles, or the deep? Fascinating, isn't it? You may learn that an eagle's eyesight is five or six times sharper than a human's. Or that snakes use their muscles and scales to push off bumpy surfaces but can't move on glass at all. Or that colorful species of fish ex[ist miles below the ocean's surface. God designed every creature. You don't have to understand it all to worship your Creator.

*God, I worship You alone. You are the maker of heaven*
*and earth. I'm so thankful for the creation I see*
*everyday that points me to the One who made it all.*

# The Very Best You

*Follow my advice. . .always treasure my*
*commands. Obey my commands and live!*
*Guard my instructions as you guard your own eyes.*

PROVERBS 7:1-2 NLT

Obedience is not a popular word today. If you're like many adult women, you don't want someone telling you what to do and who to be. You dread being quashed by another's demands. Yet when God asks you to obey His directives, He's liberating you. His guidelines help you to take care of your soul. Follow Him to become the best you can be.

*Lord, I know that obeying You leads me to freedom!*
*Your guidelines for me allow me to live in peace*
*without fear. Thank You for parenting me well.*

# Protected from Harm

*Those who obey the commands protect themselves.*
PROVERBS 19:16 NCV

You are learning to treat yourself well. You don't make a practice of behaving in self-destructive ways, nor do you sabotage your relationships or your finances. Recognizing God's authority, you choose to follow His instructions. Like all human beings, you sometimes make mistakes; but you think them through, remedy what you can, and forgive yourself. You know that when you obey God and grow, you actually are protecting yourself from harm. In this you can find comfort and joy.

*Jesus, I yield to Your will in my life. Give me the desire to obey Your words, knowing that they ultimately bring freedom and joy.*

## New Freedom

*The soul of the diligent is richly supplied.*
PROVERBS 13:4 ESV

"I have no choice in the matter." Perhaps you've uttered these words when facing a difficult decision. If so, you've probably felt the trapped sensation that accompanies this misbelief. The truth is, you do have choices. You can ask questions, research your options, consider the pros and cons, and then make a reasonable choice based on the knowledge you have at the time. By your own diligent action, that boxed-in feeling will subside and you'll enjoy new freedom.

*God, You created me with the ability to choose. What a gift! I pray that the wisdom You've given me would lead me to make choices that honor You.*

## Investigate

*The first speech in a court case is always convincing—*
*until the cross-examination starts! You may have*
*to draw straws when faced with a tough decision.*
PROVERBS 18:17–18 MSG

What you believe about a situation or person affects how you feel and what you do. That's good, because by altering your belief to correctly reflect reality, you can change how you feel and transform your follow-up action. Consequently, it's wise to investigate both sides of an issue or opportunity. Listen, see the merit in each option, and your judgmental attitudes will fade. You'll realize that several choices are acceptable and no one has the perfect answer all the time.

*Lord, help me to be wise as I make decisions about*
*circumstance and people. Remove a heart of judgment*
*from me, and fill me with Your wisdom and grace.*

# Patience and Persistence

*Patient persistence pierces through indifference;*
*gentle speech breaks down rigid defenses.*
PROVERBS 25:15 MSG

Microwave dinners, emails and Twitter posts on your cell phone, 24-7 news channels, instant messaging. We're not used to waiting for much. But when it comes to relationships, we really need patience. You can't change someone else. You can only adjust your own attitudes and behavior. But positive change takes time, whether it is you or the other person who decides to change. Be encouraged, though. Patience and persistence will pay off in the long run.

*Heavenly Father, forgive me for the times I've*
*tried to be the Holy Spirit in another person's life.*
*Remind me that only You can change people's hearts.*

## Live Today First!

*Do not boast about tomorrow, for you
do not know what a day may bring.*

PROVERBS 27:1 NIV

Remember when you were a little girl, looking forward to your family's summer vacation? You wanted to go now. Mother said, "Be patient." You couldn't wait for the next day to arrive. Living one day at a time is how you finally made it to your much-anticipated holiday. Practicing patience is like that. It's just one step at a time. You don't know exactly what tomorrow will be like. You have to live today first. So make the most of it!

*Thank You for the gift of today, Father! Let me live life to the full on this day. Help me to say what needs to be said and do what needs doing. Today.*

# Ask for Insight

*A heart at peace gives life to the body.*
PROVERBS 14:30 NIV

You are an exquisitely made woman. Your body affects your mind, your mind influences your emotions, your emotions impact your beliefs and decisions, and in turn, your choices affect your body. God made you this way. He expects you to value your body, mind, and emotions because your fluctuating hormones and chemical levels inevitably influence the way you think, feel, and react. Ask God for insight into practical and peace-filled ways to manage your variable emotions and thoughts.

*Lord, I offer my body to You as a living temple.*
*Make Your home in me. I invite You in to make*
*things new and to fill me with Your Spirit.*

## By God's Principles

*When the ways of people please the Lord, he causes
even their enemies to be at peace with them.*

PROVERBS 16:7 NRSV

God loves us all the time, whether we make good or not-so-good choices. But just like any caring parent, God isn't pleased with our rebellious behavior. He instructs us about how to interact with others for our own benefit and satisfaction. It is a fact of life that when we choose to live by God's wise principles we experience peace—even with our enemies. Make it your goal to follow God's directives and enjoy peace with others.

*I choose to trust You, Lord. Even when relationships
are hard and You've asked me to make bold moves.
I know that You see me and will direct my ways.*

# People-Pleasing

*An honest answer is like a warm hug.*
PROVERBS 24:26 MSG

Know anyone who pushes too hard to make everything, or at least something, just right? Perhaps you're the one who overachieves—and you're tired. What motivates you to continue this exhausting pattern? Maybe you're trying to avoid someone's disapproval by saying yes when you'd rather say no. God wants to protect you from overwork and burnout. Sometimes no is the most honest answer you can give. It's like giving yourself a warm hug.

*I need help practicing a healthy "no," Lord God!*
*Place a radar in my heart, alerting me to when I*
*need to be truthful and set boundaries for myself.*

## Trust His Response

*Being afraid of people can get you into trouble,*
*but if you trust the LORD, you will be safe.*

PROVERBS 29:25 NCV

Your friend wants you to do one thing. Your husband suggests something else. Both their ideas are different than what your pastor asked of you. You feel torn. You're afraid that if you do what one would like, the other person will be displeased. You get that troubling, yet familiar feeling in the pit of your stomach. You can change your people-pleasing approach. God will help you to get off this exhausting merry-go-round. Ask Him how to start the process and then trust His response.

*Remove the people-pleaser in me, Holy Spirit! Help*
*me to bring all of my decisions to You first before I say*
*yes to people who may be displeased with my choice.*

## Careful Planning

*Careful planning puts you ahead in the long run;*
*hurry and scurry puts you further behind.*
PROVERBS 21:5 MSG

When you follow God's lead in your life, is planning really necessary? Perhaps you've asked this question or heard someone voice it. Planning may seem unspiritual—like you're not really trusting God for your immediate future. Yet when you avoid making wise plans, often urgency takes over. Then you feel pressure to hurry and make it work. The good news is, careful planning reduces stress in any role: home manager, mother, volunteer, CEO, friend, or employee.

*I submit all my plans to You first, Lord. I offer*
*them with an open hand. Place a flexibility inside*
*of me to adjust things as You speak to me.*

## Next Steps

*Do your planning and prepare your
fields before building your house.*

PROVERBS 24:27 NLT

God wants you to experience the many benefits of
wise planning. Through thoughtful preparation and
open communication, your team gets on the same page.
Enthusiasm and commitment increase. Responsibilities
and duties become clear. You know who does what.
Because your schedule makes sense, that draining sense
of overwhelming tasks fades. You have space to deal with
inevitable surprises. You can measure the results. And
that creates a sense of satisfaction and accomplishment.
Now you're ready for the next big step!

*Heavenly Father, I bring all of my ideas and plans to
You. Help me to sort out what is good and life-giving.
Help me to toss out what creates chaos and despair.*

# *Pleasure!*

*The LORD has made everything for its purpose.*
PROVERBS 16:4 NRSV

Pleasure isn't the key purpose of life, but it is one of God's gifts to His children. Your five senses—hearing, seeing, touching, tasting, and smelling—are from your loving Creator and evidences that He created you with the potential to enjoy yourself, others, and His creation. The next time you take a walk around your neighborhood, consciously listen, watch, touch, taste, and sniff your surroundings. Allow yourself to sink into the pleasure of being alive.

*Help me to never take for granted all of the blessings around me, Lord. I praise You because I'm fearfully and wonderfully made!*

## Delight in His Gift

*Living wisely brings pleasure to the sensible.*
PROVERBS 10:23 NLT

God, the source of all wisdom, doesn't only love you, He likes you too. He takes pleasure in you and delights in your company. And He longs for you to find pleasure in Him as well. God freely gives wisdom to those who seek and love Him, and He wants you to delight in His gift. So relax and enjoy playing and working today at your job, with your family, in your alone time, and with your friends.

*It does my heart good to know how You delight in me, Lord. As I delight in my children, You delight in seeing me enjoy Your everyday blessings. Thank You!*

# Silent Worship

*Be zealous for the fear of the Lord all the day.*
PROVERBS 23:17 NKJV

There is no one like God. Never has been. Never will be. He keeps the earth balancing on its axis. He gives breath to every living creature. He promises eternal life to each believing soul. He cares. He provides. He protects. He comforts. He never makes a mistake. And that's just the beginning of who He is. God inspires awe, respect, and reverence, and this leads to spontaneous praise—all day long. Go ahead. Honor Him with your silent worship.

*God, You are so good to me! I praise You for allowing me this life. . .and for living daily in me. Show me how to honor You in everything.*

## Praise Him!

*There is no wisdom, no insight,*
*no plan that can succeed against the Lord.*
PROVERBS 21:30 NIV

God is the ultimate question and the ultimate answer. No plan is more important than He is. His wisdom has no rival. All beneficial insight originates in Him. He created music and gives it as a loving gift to His children. He generously shares His creativity, knowledge, and joy with you, your family, your friends, your fellow church members, your coworkers, your heroes, and your government leaders. God will never stop giving, loving, saving, caring. Don't you want to praise Him?

*Thank You for music, Lord. It draws my heart in*
*as nothing else does. I worship You with music,*
*with my words, with my heart, and with my life.*

## Safe with Him

*The name of the LORD is a strong fortress;*
*the godly run to him and are safe.*
PROVERBS 18:10 NLT

Stop. Pause. Breathe. Take a moment to contemplate how big God is. How He orchestrates nature by His power. That right now He is with you and with your friend across the ocean. How He never sleeps yet doesn't tire. Think how much He loves you. How He sent Jesus to prove that love. Let your heart run to Him. Sense His strong arms holding you. Pray, telling Him what you're feeling at this moment. You're safe with Him.

*Lord, You are my place of true safety. I run to You,*
*and I know You can handle everything I bring.*
*Thank You for Your great love and protection.*

# Connected

*The prayer of the upright is His delight.*
PROVERBS 15:8 NKJV

Perhaps you know what it feels like to be ignored or cut off when trying to talk to someone you care about. A spouse? Your father? Close friend? Boss? Child? It's hurtful—even maddening—to be disregarded. But God's not like that. He delights in listening to you. He knows you're not perfect. Still, He sees your desire to connect with Him. He looks at you through the sacrifice of His Son, Jesus. So drop any hesitancy. Go ahead. Pray.

*Heavenly Father, thank You for always listening.*
*I pray that You would help me begin to learn*
*how to have two-way conversations with You.*

# Worthwhile Results

*She senses the worth of her work.*
PROVERBS 31:18 MSG

The word *pride* has contrasting meanings. For example, when you hear a pastor say, "Pride alienates us from God," you may want to run in the opposite direction. Then someone introduces a respected Bible teacher with "She takes pride in what she's discovered and accomplished." So what's appropriate? Both. Although you don't wish to be arrogant, you do want to partner with God for your own growth and then accept the worthwhile results with dignity, gratitude, and celebration.

*Lord, I confess the times I have been proud*
*with a haughty attitude. Change my heart*
*to humbly see the worth in everything I do.*

## Surrender All

*The wise listen to advice.*

PROVERBS 12:15 NRSV

Negative pride is an enemy of the heart and can lead to exhaustion and burnout. It whispers, "I have a better idea, God." Sometimes it looks arrogantly brash. Other times, pride appears selfless and nice, but it tries too hard to fix everyone and play peacemaker at any cost. Both approaches leave little room for God's intervention, because pride has everything under control. Relief comes when we admit our need, listen to wise and gentle advice, and surrender it all to God.

*Please rid my heart of negative pride, Lord God.*
*Show me the areas of my life that I've yet to surrender*
*fully to You, and soften my heart for change.*

# Rearranged Priorities

*The beginning of wisdom is this: Get wisdom.*
*Though it cost all you have, get understanding.*

PROVERBS 4:7 NIV

Honoring God lays the foundation for building a life of wisdom. If you want to be wise, arrange your calendar to include time for God. You might have to say no to something in order to say yes to that Bible study or quiet time praying and reading God's Word or meeting with a spiritual mentor or attending worship service or keeping a spiritual journal. Though it may cost you, rearranging your priorities will help you to gain wisdom.

*Lord, please help me to be wise when it comes to*
*my schedule. Give me a discerning mind so that*
*I know when to say no and to protect my yes.*

## In Training

*If you make Insight your priority, and won't take no for an answer...before you know it Fear-of-GOD will be yours; you'll have come upon the Knowledge of God.*

PROVERBS 2:3–5 MSG

Does it feel like becoming a truly wise and godly woman is too far out of your reach? Be encouraged. You're probably already on the path to wisdom. Do you pray for God's help to understand His Word? Are you seeking an intimate relationship with Jesus? Do you desire greater knowledge about finances, healthy relationships, and your work life? Is your view of God's power and love deepening? Yes? Then you're a wise-woman-in-training.

*Thank You for teaching me and speaking to me, Lord. I can feel Your guidance at work in my life. Encourage my heart with Your truth.*

# In Truth

*Trusting the LORD leads to prosperity.*
PROVERBS 28:25 NLT

A teacher asked her students for their definition of *prosperity*. Various responses were shouted across the classroom. Good fortune, success, money, wealth, riches, abundance, financial gain, profits. Several dictionaries define the word *prosperity* as "a profitable, flourishing, or successful situation, particularly in monetary matters." Wise King Solomon's definition of prosperity probably included *shalom*: "peace, safety, well-being." When you trust God and follow His lead, you receive a personal sense of well-being. You can rest, live, and work in that truth.

*Build deeper trust in me, Lord God.*
*Please increase my faith as I follow You*
*and witness Your faithfulness in my life.*

# Great Respect

*Better a little with the fear of the*
*LORD than great wealth with turmoil.*

PROVERBS 15:16 NIV

If you listen to national news stories, you may notice that having lots of money doesn't guarantee contentment, perfect bodies, happy children, secure marriages, or stable investments. Although prosperity doesn't automatically lead to trouble, neither does it secure inner peace, health, or joy. In fact, reality indicates that problems abound when individuals strive solely for financial gain. Of much greater value is your personal relationship with the Creator God, the One who never changes and is worthy of your complete respect.

*Lord, please help me to be content with all that*
*You've given me—whether a little or a lot.*
*Your presence in my life is worth everything.*

## Beside You—Always

*No need to panic over alarms or surprises, or predictions
that doomsday's just around the corner, because GOD will
be right there with you; he'll keep you safe and sound.*
PROVERBS 3:25-26 MSG

Everyone feels fearful at times. What if I lose my job?
What if the terrorists strike again? What if I get sick
and can't take care of my family? None of us want these
things to happen. Yet when we focus on the what-ifs,
rationality and common sense often go out the window.
God, the wisdom giver, is also your protector. He is right
beside you always. You can trust Him with this moment—
and with your future.

*Forgive me for worrying about the future, Lord.
You tell me that it's senseless to do so and
rids my life of joy in the present moment.*

## Safe with Him

*"Every promise of God proves true;*
*he protects everyone who runs to him for help."*

PROVERBS 30:5 MSG

God is true to His word. It's not in His nature to deceive or play games with you. He provided for the needs of Abraham, Moses, and Jesus' mother and earthly father. And He'll provide for your needs too. God loves you a lot. He keeps all His promises to you. When you come to Him, telling Him about your concerns, asking for His protection, He meets you with open arms. With Him you are safe.

*Lord, I trust Your will and plan for my life.*
*You will be with me and see me through anything*
*that comes my way. I put my whole trust in You.*

# Prudence

*The gullible believe anything they're told;*
*the prudent sift and weigh every word.*

PROVERBS 14:15 MSG

Try this toothpaste and you'll dazzle them with whiter teeth. Splash on this perfume and you'll have more dates. Follow these steps and double your income. Apply this lotion and say goodbye to crow's feet. But is it all true? Perhaps. Perhaps not. But you can find out. You don't have to fall victim to false promises and worry. The wise woman of God asks questions, researches her options, sifts through the maze, and then takes intentional action.

*I continue to pray for wisdom, Lord. I want*
*to be wise not so that others see me as that,*
*but so I can follow You wholeheartedly.*

## Thoughtful Decisions

*Wise realists plant their feet on the ground.*
PROVERBS 14:18 MSG

Your head's in the clouds!" If you heard this as a child when you were just trying to have fun, maybe you thought you should stop dreaming, come down to earth, and be boring. If you were praised for not keeping your head in the clouds, you probably learned to put your nose to the grindstone and avoid pleasure. But being a wise realist doesn't mean either extreme. You can make thoughtful decisions about your reality and still enjoy life.

*Heavenly Father, I ask that You place a sense of balance in my life. Help to me to work hard and make time for joyful rest and recreation too.*

## Blessing and Joy

*Drink water from your own well—*
*share your love only with your [husband.]*
PROVERBS 5:15 NLT

Whether you're a wife or not, you've probably noticed that infidelity is growing, or at least people are talking about it more. It's difficult to live in a culture where sexual flirtation and innuendo has become just another way to say hello. Contrary to what movies, television, and the internet may suggest, the wisest approach to pleasing the opposite sex is to stay true to yourself and demonstrate respect. There you'll find blessing—and joy.

*I want to trust Your words above all, Lord. Including what*
*You have to say about my sexuality and relationships.*
*I honor Your thoughts above the cultural norms.*

## Pure Motives

*Mixed motives twist life into tangles;*
*pure motives take you straight down the road.*
PROVERBS 21:8 MSG

Remember that game of Twister you used to play? Your arms and legs got twisted up with themselves and everyone else's. So you got confused and couldn't tell where to go next. Maybe that's how you feel about your life journey. If so, ask yourself: What do I really want? Who or what am I doing this for? Answering these questions helps you to start over with pure motives, leaving any hidden agendas behind.

*Lord, I bring all of my life goals, plans, and ideas*
*to Your throne. Help me to sort out what I'm doing*
*and for whom. Place Your desires in my heart.*

## He'll Walk with You

*"Are you confused about life, don't know what's going on?
Come with me.... Leave your impoverished confusion
and live! Walk up the street to a life with meaning."*

PROVERBS 9:4–6 MSG

God isn't put off by your confusion. Tell Him how you're feeling and what you're perplexed about—even if it doesn't make sense to you. He will give you purpose and meaning as you become more acquainted with His wise direction. You don't have to wait until you understand what your problems are before you come to Him. He'll walk with you as you determine what steps to take, resources to contact, and decisions to make.

*Remind me how real You are, Lord. Sometimes
I forget that You are the answer to all of my
questions. . .and the source of my strength and joy.*

# Purpose-Filled Life

*It's through me, Lady Wisdom, that your life
deepens, and the years of your life ripen.
Live wisely and wisdom will permeate your life.*

PROVERBS 9:11–12 MSG

I t's never too late to discover more about your giftedness
and personality. No matter what your age or season of life,
all your experiences (your family, education, jobs, talents,
and disappointments) matter. They merge together to make
you the unique person that you are. God wants to use your
story wisely for your fulfillment and His glory. Be intentional
about seeking wisdom, and partner with God for a purpose-
filled rest of your life.

*Thank You for my life's story, heavenly Father.
Even the difficult times have made me who I
am and are important to Your master plan.*

# Rewarding Relationships

*As iron sharpens iron, so a friend sharpens a friend.*
PROVERBS 27:17 NLT

Have you ever tried to cut a friend's hair with styling scissors that had dull blades? Or slice through a piece of steak with an unsharpened knife? It's frustrating, and the results are less than satisfying. Yet when you rub the dull blade against a separate piece of iron, it works better. Likewise, when you interact with a good friend, sharing honest feedback, encouraging one another's growth, you each become wiser. How rewarding is that?

*Lord, I continue to ask that You cultivate good, healthy relationships in my life. I ask for one or two good friends who understand and affirm my heart for Your will.*

# Honor Your Relationships

*Good news from far away is
like cold water to the thirsty.*

PROVERBS 25:25 NLT

Your close friend loves you. You support and love her too, whether she's hurting or celebrating. You can think of ways in which you're different. (She likes to eat organic food; you don't. You have four brothers; she's an only child.) But it doesn't matter. When you're apart, you miss her. You've learned how refreshing it feels to stay connected, even though it takes focused planning. And you just know God loves it when you honor your relationships.

*Heavenly Father, I pray that You would help
me to become a wise, healthy, good friend.
I want to honor You as I honor my friends.*

## Breathe Easy

*She is clothed with strength and dignity,*
*and she laughs without fear of the future.*
PROVERBS 31:25 NLT

Take it easy! Lighten up! Chill! Mellow out! You wish you could. But there's so much going on. You feel the pressure. Job worries; money, health, and family problems; that approaching deadline—sometimes all at once. Although you'll never be completely stress free in this chaotic world, you can ask God for wisdom and discernment. By trusting Him to work in and through you, you'll find strength to meet your daily challenges. Then you can breathe easier about what you face.

*Lord, when life gets chaotic, remind me of my*
*deep need for You. Delight me with some comic*
*relief, and lighten my load as I trust in You.*

## You Deserve It

*"First pay attention to me, and then relax.*
*Now you can take it easy—you're in good hands."*
PROVERBS 1:33 MSG

Maybe you believe you need to stay on constant alert and be just a little tense in order to prove how much you care. After all, doing God's work is serious business, right? Yet you don't have to solve all your friends' and family's dilemmas. When you try too hard to make it all just right, you lose your sense of joy. And that's no fun. God wants you to take it easy. So relax. You deserve it.

*Forgive me when I try to take Your job, Lord.*
*I cannot fix anyone, including myself.*
*Help me to relax as I put my trust in You.*

# Wise Follower of God

---

*Do not let loyalty and faithfulness forsake you. . . .*
*So you will find favor and good repute*
*in the sight of God and of people.*

PROVERBS 3:3–4 NRSV

How important is a good reputation? Some insist it must be prized at all costs. Others say it's more crucial to develop good character than a stellar reputation. But God values both. According to the Bible, Jesus increased in wisdom and favor with others and with His Father. Although you can't guarantee that everyone will like you all the time, you can follow Jesus' example and live so that you're gaining a reputation as a wise follower of God.

---

*Heavenly Father, I ask that You purify my heart,*
*my actions, and my motives. Let everything I*
*do be done for Your glory and not my own.*

## More Rewarding

*A good name is more desirable than great riches;*
*to be esteemed is better than silver or gold.*

PROVERBS 22:1 NIV

Building a godly reputation takes time. You become known as a genuinely wise woman by seeking God first—spending time with Him, sharing your thoughts and desires, reading His Word, and listening for His Spirit's response in your heart. Not with fanfare, but in a quiet "Here I am, Lord" way. You become amazed by Him, and it shows in how you treat others. Living this way is more rewarding than being renowned for great wealth or success.

*I pray that I will live my life in a way that You*
*will be esteemed, Lord. That because of my life,*
*others will see and know that You are good.*

# Happy Medium

*A wise youth harvests in the summer.*
PROVERBS 10:5 NLT

"You owe me," says someone who wants you to finish his report and cover for him. You're already overcommitted, but you agree to do it. It's the story of two extremes: tired, irresponsible person versus exhausted woman with an exaggerated sense of responsibility. Both of you miss the joy of a job (and life) well done. But there's a happy medium. It is God's wise plan that each should be responsible for their own tasks, mistakes, and growth. When someone's in need, help them, but try not to shoulder the whole burden.

*Lord, I ask for a strong sense of discernment as I carry other people's burdens. I want to help in healthy ways, not enable their poor choices.*

# Responsibility for Growth

*Just as a door turns on its hinges,*
*so a lazybones turns back over in bed.*
PROVERBS 26:14 MSG

If you put off completing a project, you might call yourself lazy. But often procrastination is simply covert perfectionism. You believe you should do it all just right but can't (because only God is perfect), so you're disappointed in yourself. You try, stop, try again, and give up. It's like swinging in and out without making progress. The truth is, God loves you and gifted you. You can take responsibility for your own growth. You don't have to be perfect.

*God, I ask for a greater sense of responsibility*
*for my growth. Thank You for my gifts and abilities.*
*I submit them to You to use for Your glory.*

## Vital

*If you sit down, you will not be afraid.*

PROVERBS 3:24 NRSV

God loves it when you take a break from your work and responsibilities to sit and relax for a while. Human beings cannot live outside their limitations. God alone is limitless. As a wise woman, you will recognize your human need for relief-filled rest and respite times. Don't worry that you'll be unproductive if you pause to rejuvenate. Both work and rest are not only important, but vital for healthy living.

*Heavenly Father, place a wise understanding of my need for rest in this busy life. Give me the courage and ability to take time for vital rest in my life.*

## *Release Your Cares*

*Laziness brings on deep sleep,*
*and the shiftless go hungry.*
PROVERBS 19:15 NIV

In case you're concerned that taking a day off or a full-fledged vacation will characterize you as lazy or irresponsible, here's a tip for you: one afternoon, one week, one month, or in some cases, one year of respite will not an idle woman make! A truly lazy person makes idleness a way of life. You can, with God's help, release your cares and worries and enjoy a little time off.

*Thank You, Lord, for vacation time! Help me*
*to thoroughly enjoy a time of rest, rejuvenation,*
*and relaxation with my family—weekly and yearly.*

# Mercy Raft

*People who conceal their sins will not prosper, but if they
confess and turn from them, they will receive mercy.*

Proverbs 28:13 nlt

To use a common cliché, we're all in the same boat.
Every one of us needs God. Pretending you're in total
control and have no spiritual need just pushes God away.
Still, it may feel like you're giving up who you are and
throwing yourself into the ocean without a life jacket if
you release yourself and your offenses to God. Actually,
the opposite is true. Coming clean before God allows Him
to throw you a mercy raft.

*I long to be cleansed by You, Lord. I long to
live and walk in truth and freedom. Thank You
for all You've done to offer mercy and grace to me.*

## Bull's-Eye

*No one can say, "I am innocent;*
*I have never done anything wrong."*

PROVERBS 20:9 NCV

Human beings, although created and treasured by God, are just not good enough to hit the bull's-eye of God's perfection. It's a dilemma because we long to know our Creator. The good news is we can quit working so frantically to be something that's impossible. Jesus hit the bull's-eye for us. His work on the cross makes us right with God. Ask God to show you more about what Jesus did for you.

*It's all about You and for You, Jesus. Let my*
*heart be set on this truth. I live in darkness*
*without You. You are the light of my heart.*

# Satisfaction

*The fear of the LORD leads to life,*
*and [she] who has it will abide in satisfaction.*
PROVERBS 19:23 NKJV

What ties you in knots, robbing your sense of well-being? Whatever it is that keeps you feeling trapped in a cramped little box and gasping for air isn't from God. Maybe you only feel like this occasionally. Perhaps you're accustomed to it. Either way, you don't have to stay in that box. God will open the lid and release you to freedom. Give Him your life, experience His power to free your soul, and enjoy the satisfaction He longs to give.

*Lord, guide me as I step out of all the unhealthy boxes I've ever known. Some are long-lived. Give me the courage, faith, and hope to trust in You for freedom.*

## Heart for Others

*An appetite for good brings much satisfaction.*
PROVERBS 13:25 MSG

God—and all He is and does—portrays goodness. He is perfectly loving, kind, forgiving, fair, patient, and good. And although you aren't (It's a relief to admit, isn't it?), He shares Himself with you when you believe in His Son, Jesus. Then you grow hungry to know Him more. He supplies your inner longing and gives you a heart of love for others. As you develop a healthy appetite to do good in this world, you will experience deep satisfaction.

*Lord, please plant a deep desire in my heart to know You more and to want Your ways in my thoughts and actions. Grant me a loving and kind heart for others.*

## *Self Care*

---

*Your kindness will reward you,*
*but your cruelty will destroy you.*
PROVERBS 11:17 NLT

What do you do when a friend shares her exhaustion or discouragement with you? Because you care, you probably listen, acknowledge her current reality, tell her how you appreciate her, remind her of recent accomplishments, or suggest she give herself a break. Today, try sharing the same responses with yourself. Harsh words rarely motivate others—yourself included. When you're kind to yourself, you flourish inside and grow into becoming the woman God designed you to be.

---

*Change my thinking to be more kind and encouraging*
*to myself, Lord. Help me to bless my body and not*
*curse it by unhealthy thoughts and actions.*

# God-Given Responsibility

*Above all else, guard your heart,
for everything you do flows from it.*

PROVERBS 4:23 NIV

How you feel physically affects how you think—and vice versa. Your thinking impacts your emotions which influence your actions. God chose to design you this way. Ancient scholars understood that when you protect your heart, you're actually caring for your entire being—body, mind, and soul. It's your God-given responsibility and privilege to physically, emotionally, spiritually, and mentally safeguard yourself. Wise self-care honors God.

*Remind me that my body is Your temple,
Lord God. Give me the wisdom to take
care of myself in wise and healthy ways.*

## Sweet Sleep

---

*Hold on to wisdom and good sense. Don't let*
*them out of your sight.... When you lie down,*
*you won't be afraid.... You will sleep in peace.*

PROVERBS 3:21, 24 NCV

Keep your room cool and dark. No caffeine before bedtime. Don't watch violent TV while trying to fall asleep. Listen to calming music. Contract and relax each muscle until your body feels less tense. Take a warm bath. These are a few of the instructions experts give to those who have trouble falling asleep at night. They often work too. Probably because they're based on good sense, research, and acquired knowledge. Just like God's Word advised many years ago!

---

*Draw my heart to Yours as I close out each day, Lord.*
*I put my hope and trust in You as I go to sleep at night.*
*I can rest in peace because You are awake.*

## Good Counsel

*Follow your father's good advice; don't wander
off from your mother's teachings. Wrap yourself
in them. . . . Wherever you walk, they'll guide you;
whenever you rest, they'll guard you.*

PROVERBS 6:20-22 MSG

What did your father and mother tell—and show—you about working, taking care of yourself, and managing your life? Any good counsel you received from your parents (or other wise mentors) is worth remembering and heeding. God uses their past input to give you a foundation for wise living now. If your current sleeping and waking routines are off-kilter, ask God to help you implement some wise advice from your past so you can enjoy your present life more.

*Heavenly Father, help me to be wise in the way I take care of myself. I know everything that matters to me is important to You too. Thank You for caring for me!*

## Careful Speech

*The good acquire a taste for helpful conversation; bullies push and shove their way through life. Careful words make for a careful life; careless talk may ruin everything.*

PROVERBS 13:2–3 MSG

What God created for pleasure and benefit can turn against you. God created food for your nourishment, yet too much or too little causes problems. Friendships add meaning to life, but unwise relationship choices bring unnecessary pain. God blesses you with work, yet job/mission obsession often sparks burnouts. Similarly, words connect you with others, but reckless speech alienates. The good news: God doesn't leave you to wander carelessly through life. He gives you direction. Ask for what you need today.

*God, I come to You to ask for help with my thoughts and words. Show me how to take every thought captive before I speak with others. Help me to be a wise conversationalist.*

# Wise Methods

*The speech of a good person clears the air.*
PROVERBS 10:32 MSG

One way you can discover how to speak wisely is to examine Jesus' life and communication style. What did He say to friends? To enemies? How did He initiate conversation? Jesus met people in the moment, at the point of their immediate need. He asked them what they wanted. He listened. Often His straightforward responses cleared the air between them. You can relax because you'll never communicate perfectly like Jesus, but you can observe His wise methods and learn.

*Lord Jesus, please give me courage to speak wisely, lovingly, and truthfully with others. Help me to be authentic and yet full of grace. Lead me in this, Jesus.*

# Teachability

*Whoever heeds instruction is on the path to life.*
PROVERBS 10:17 NRSV

Sometimes it's hard to take the time to heed instruction, although it would help you to manage your current season more effectively. At your job, there's necessary training about new tech equipment. There's advice about health issues and information about how to better interact with friends and family. It's tempting to pretend you already know it all. Yet as a teachable woman of God, you can admit your need, accept sensible advice, and learn practical tools that will enhance your life today.

*Lord, open my mind and heart to accept wise advice
and helpful instruction. Give me a teachable and
amiable spirit as I work with others, Father.*

# Scripture Index

Try *3-Minute Devotions from the Psalms:*
*Inspiration for Women*

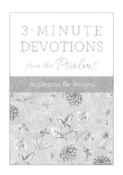

Written especially for women, this devotional
packs a powerful dose of comfort, encouragement,
and inspiration from the Psalms into just-right-
sized readings for women on the go. Each day's
reading meets women right where they are—and is
complemented by a relevant scripture and prayer.
Paperback / 978-1-68322-400-6 / $4.99